SOUL SURFER

DEVOTIONS

SOUL SURFER

DEVOTIONS

BETHANY HAMILTON
with Ann Byle

THOMAS NELSON
Since 1798

NASHVILLE   DALLAS   MEXICO CITY   RIO DE JANEIRO

Published in Nashville, Tennessee, by Thomas Nelson. Thomas Nelson is a
registered trademark of Thomas Nelson, Inc.

Written by Ann Byle.
Cover design by Studio Gearbox.
Cover photo by Noah Hamilton, noahhamiltonphoto.com.
Page design by Lori Lynch.

Thomas Nelson, Inc., titles may be purchased in bulk for educational,
business, fund-raising, or sales promotional use. For information, please
e-mail SpecialMarkets@ThomasNelson.com.

Library of Congress Control Number: 20-06011602

ISBN: 978-1-4003-1723-3

Printed in the United States of America

11 12 13 14 15 RRD 6 5 4

Mfr: RR Donnelley / Crawfordsville, IN / June 2011 / PPO 122834

This book is dedicated to Jesus Christ, who has given me the most wonderful friends and family and who loves me with an undying love.

—Bethany

Acknowledgments

From the bottom of my heart I thank
my heavenly Father and Savior, Jesus Christ. I am
grateful to everybody who has helped me on this
book: Ann Byle for coauthoring it with me; Kate Etue
and Michelle Burke, my editors; Tim Beals; Thomas
Nelson; and World Vision. Special thanks to my good
friend and sister-in-law, Becky Hamilton, who helped
me write and organize my thoughts. This book
never would have been written if it weren't for your
dedication.

I want to acknowledge the "Bethany Team": my
management—Dad, Mom, Noah, Timmy, and Becky—
for all your hard work and full support in every area of
my life, and Roy Hofstetter and Andy Smith for helping
us get our feet off the ground. Without all of you, my
life would be much more difficult; and because of your
diligence, God has been able to do great things through
our lives and ministry.

I want to recognize my church, North Shore
Christian Fellowship, and all my friends I grew up with
at youth group, whom I would practically die without!
You guys kept me grounded. Also, my pastor and his
wife, Steve and Trisha Thompson; and my youth leader

while growing up, best friend, and role model, Sarah Hill—you encourage me when I get overwhelmed and help me to remember God's overall plan! So important!

I would also like to thank Rick Bundschuh, who helped me write my first book, *Soul Surfer*, because it opened up so many doors and paved the way for this book.

To all my other friends and family, thank you for the love and support you've shown me throughout my life!

—Bethany

Where Am I Now?

At Home

Well, it's been more than seven years since I lost my arm in a shark attack, and my life has changed so much since then. I've seen God answer a lot of prayers in my own life and in other people's lives. I've traveled all over the world and have been able to see that God is working in places that most people have never even heard of.

But at the same time, some things in my life are pretty much the same! I'm still living on the island of Kauai, Hawaii, in the same home with my parents, Tom and Cheri. I turned twenty-one on February 8, 2011, and have grown to the height of five foot eleven! The main reason I still live at home is because I travel so much. I'm usually traveling more than 50 percent of the year. So it's kind of pointless to get my own place at this time in life.

My oldest brother, Noah, got married in 2009 to my friend and personal assistant, Becky. He is still my main photographer and shoots weddings, portraits, and lots of other photo jobs; and he helps manage my surfing. And my brother Timmy, the bodyboarder, is working as a camera PA in the television/filmmaking industry. He still shoots video of me and does other video-related work on the side. Both brothers worked on *Soul Surfer,* the feature film about my story.

That brings me to some big news: a major motion picture is coming out about my life! It's so weird to even be saying that. It's based on my book *Soul Surfer*, and it's being released by Sony Pictures Entertainment! It's so exciting yet nerve-racking to have this movie come out. I did some of the stunt surfing for my character, which was really fun! The movie has a great team of actors and a great story (I'm a little biased, ha ha!), and I think it's going to be a really positive film.

I have also had the privilege of being invited to speak in front of congregations and groups of all sizes to share my story. I've been to churches, community events, business conferences, schools, and other sorts of events. Though speaking isn't quite my forte yet, I have had moments of really feeling comfortable on the stage, sharing my heart during my Q&A sessions. It's something I'm definitely considering doing more of in the future, but for now I'm going to focus on surfing!

On the Board

As far as surfing goes, I began competing full-time on the Association of Surfing Professionals (ASP) circuit in 2008. The ASP has two tiers of competition: the Star Series and the World Tour. I primarily surf the Star Series, with the goal of qualifying for the World Tour—which is comprised of the top seventeen female surfers in the world. So far, I have come *really close* to qualifying and have placed in the top twenty every year.

Now that I'm a pro surfer, it's definitely important that I be a serious professional athlete. As I began taking my training to the next level, talking to the experts, and learning more about the human body, I began to get serious about my nutrition in addition to my fitness. My family has always been pretty healthy eaters, or so I thought! I have spent a lot of time in the past few years soaking up information about how our bodies were designed by God to function and about how to help them do that in a world of processed foods, which can lead to problems and diseases. I have since developed a habit of eating that suits my body's needs, and I would encourage you all to do the same.

Aside from having a good nutritional diet, I have been doing a lot of physical training. As you can imagine, this is highly important for any professional athlete. In my case, since I have only one arm, I needed to work on my spinal alignment first, getting "straight, then strong!" My trainers and I have worked out a program for me to help my spine stay in alignment, and they've developed specific exercises to help me in my surfing.

I also work with a few surf coaches who focus specifically on my technique, maneuvers, overall performance, and competition strategy. I love the constant challenge to improve and push my limits. It's critical for me to be doing that because the other women surfers are really good these days, and we all have to continue to raise the bar!

With My God

Spiritually, I'd be bummed if I couldn't report growth in the past few years. I have definitely been growing—and not always by choice! Sometimes in life you get forced into a new thing, and it demands spiritual growth, and that's okay. It's great, in fact!

The Bible speaks about this in James 1:2–4: "My brothers and sisters, when you have many kinds of troubles, you should be full of joy, because you know that these troubles test your faith, and this will give you patience. Let your patience show itself perfectly in what you do. Then you will be perfect and complete and will have everything you need."

Another good passage is Romans 5:3–5: "We also have joy with our troubles, because we know that these troubles produce patience. And patience produces character, and character produces hope. And this hope will never disappoint us, because God has poured out his love to fill our hearts. He gave us his love through the Holy Spirit, whom God has given to us."

One of the challenges I've faced, honestly, is being bold about sharing the gospel. I've been committed to giving glory to God at all times, but it's a little harder to be direct with your family, friends, or strangers about their relationships with God (or lack thereof). But one of the primary things God has called us to do as followers of him is to spread his love by helping people meet Jesus and become his disciples.

A lot of my friends have moved away and gone

off to college or work. As a result, I've kind of lost that tight support group of Christian friends I had while in junior high and high school. It's been a weird transition because it's easy to rely on others (your friends and family) for spiritual accountability and encouragement. It's definitely been a test for my faith in some ways, because when you don't have that safety group, you have to step out and be bold in your faith on your own. "Loning" it is a lot different than when you have that close group of Christian friends around you. And it has made me really need to understand what I believe and why.

I would like to encourage everyone never to be afraid to follow Jesus. Prayerfully live your life, dig deep into God's Word, and strap on your surf leash, because you're headed for a life of adventure in Jesus. He'll accomplish more than you could ever ask for or even imagine through your life!

Aloha,
Bethany

God Has a Plan!

I didn't plan on losing my left arm in a shark attack on October 31, 2003. I didn't plan on having to learn to surf all over again, and I certainly didn't plan on becoming famous. I never thought I'd write a book, or throw out the first pitch at a New York Yankees baseball game, or talk to people all over the world who have lost limbs in wars and accidents.

One thing I did plan on doing was whatever God wanted me to do. I wanted my plan to be his plan, no matter what. In fact, one of my favorite verses, Jeremiah 29:11, talks about the plans God has for those who follow him. God put his plan into action in my life in a dramatic way, yet I'm thrilled to have any opportunity to tell people about him because sometimes God uses us in small ways too.

Maybe you've had something happen in your life you didn't plan on: Your parents divorced or someone you loved died. Maybe you've gotten sick or injured or lost your home to a natural disaster such as a hurricane. Guess what? It's all part of God's plan, and he'll use you through it if you're willing.

Willingness means letting God's plan become your own, whether it's losing an arm in a shark attack or simply listening to his voice.

"For I know the plans I have for you," declares the LORD, "plans to prosper you and not to harm you, plans to give you hope and a future." (Jeremiah 29:11)

Different Words, One Language

Surfers have their own language to
describe the sport. For example, *sketched out* means
being too scared to take off on a wave, *grommet* or *grom*
is a young surfer, and *tubed* means riding deep inside
the barrel of the wave. Skateboarders, stage actors,
photographers, and computer whizzes have their own
languages as well.

Christians have a special language too. Sure, we
may use different words in our worship services or
sing to different music. We use different translations
of the Bible and may even worship at different times
of the day. But our common language is our love for
Jesus.

The Bible says that people will know we are
followers of God by our love for one another. Sometimes
we get so caught up in our daily lives and activities and
what *I* need to do. We become self-centered, forgetting
all about loving the people around us.

For you, this love might mean being nice to the
girl who doesn't like you and talks behind your back,
tolerating your younger brother or sister for a night so
your parents can go on a date, handing out food and
blankets at a homeless shelter, or befriending a person
at school who has no friends. Some ways that I like to
show love for others include encouraging people who

have lost limbs, giving money to support missionaries, and talking to people about Jesus. What can you do to turn your religion into the language called *love*?

> "All people will know that you are my followers if you love each other." (John 13:35)

The Big "What If"

It might be easy to ask myself, "What if I hadn't gone surfing that Halloween morning?" Or, "What if I had been too scared to surf again?" The problem with these questions is that they keep me from asking the more important question, which is, "What does God want me to do?"

You probably do it too: "What if I hadn't gone to that party and had those beers?" "What if I hadn't made that nasty comment to my friend?" "What if I hadn't skipped church to go to the mall?" Or, "What if I had just spent time reading the Bible instead of sleeping in?"

It's easy to get caught up in those "what if" questions. It's easy to spend so much time in the past, beating yourself up over some bad decisions, that you forget that God has work for you to do. He put you where you are, he forgives you, and he has a plan for you. God tells us to put our faith in him into action (James 2:17). For me it means doing what God created me to do and love—surfing, using the opportunities God has given me to talk about him, helping others, and learning more about God and his plan for me.

If "what if" questions are stopping you, ask for God's help in putting them behind you. Then grab hold of your faith, and get busy!

> Just as a person's body that does not have a spirit is dead, so faith that does nothing is dead! (James 2:26)

Decisions, Decisions

Are you good at making decisions? While you're a teenager, you have to make some of your first important ones—about your faith, your morals, your college plans. It can mean a lot of pressure for someone whose biggest decisions, up until a few years ago, centered around which pizza toppings to order.

So how do we make sure that our choices are the right ones? The most important way is to seek God's wisdom and direction. You can do that through prayer and studying the Bible. Another good thing to do is get as much information as you can. If you've got college questions, research schools and careers yourself, and don't be afraid to pick the brains of your guidance counselors and parents. Faith questions? First, search for the answers within your Bible. You can also get answers from a leader at your church or, again, your parents. Trusted adults have a lot of wisdom to offer.

Most importantly, don't forget to take your choices to God. He wants to hear you, and he wants to help. And he always makes the right decision.

> "Come now, and let us reason together," says the Lord. (Isaiah 1:18 NKJV)

Freedom

Got any bad habits you'd like to be free of? Like biting your nails, whining, or chewing on your hair? I have a bad habit of not looking people in the eye when I talk to them. I also leave stuff all over the floor of my bedroom, which makes me frustrated living in a messy bedroom. But it feels great when I pick up my room. And I'm a lot happier when I can actually find things.

Bad habits can be annoying, that's for sure. The worse the habit, the more it controls us. But isn't it great to be free of bad habits—when you stop chewing your hair or overeating or saying "like" all the time?

It also feels great to be free from sin. Just as you can break a bad habit, you can break the habit of sin. You can stop letting it control you by turning that sin over to Jesus. Jesus died to clear away our sinful hearts, to clean up the habit of sin we all are born with. It's not like you are never going to sin again; it's that sin doesn't control your life anymore.

Just as that messy bedroom habit has controlled me, sin controls all of us. Jesus, however, gives us freedom from a sinful heart. What a great habit to break!

> We know that our old life died with Christ on the cross so that our sinful selves would have no power over us and we would not be slaves to sin. Anyone who has died is made free from sin's control. (Romans 6:6–7)

No Worries!

Have you ever seen Simba, Timon, and
Pumba singing "Hakuna Matata" in *The Lion King*?
Simba liked the idea of never having to worry about
anything ever again. This seemed great after he
thought he'd killed his dad, then abandoned his family
and friends.

I'm sure you have worries and fears too. I know I
do. I worry that I won't do well in a surfing contest or
that I'll get hurt. I worry about my family and about my
friends making bad choices. Maybe you worry about
whether your outfit looks stupid, failing an algebra
test, your mom and dad getting a divorce, or your
grandma getting sick.

God tells us to hand over our worries to him
because he'll carry them for us (Matthew 11:28–29). It's
sort of like handing him a whole backpack full of rocks
you've been carrying around for months. It's not as if
you immediately never worry again, but God takes the
heavy burden of worry away so it doesn't weigh you
down. He wants to do this for you and eagerly waits for
you to give him your burdens. Tell God you're giving
him everything you worry about. The more you get to
know him through his Word, the easier it is to trust
him. Because with God, there really are no worries.

Give all your worries to him, because he cares about you.
(1 Peter 5:7)

Just a Thought

Ever notice how bad thoughts randomly pop into your mind? "I'm worthless." "No one could ever love me." "I should just give up; I'll never make it." Or maybe you think something bad about someone else. Don't worry. It happens to all of us. We just need to recognize where those thoughts come from and learn what to do when they come. Bad thoughts like these come straight from the devil, who's trying to get you to sin. But you don't have to let him get his way.

In my daily life, I have to disregard the thoughts that enter my mind that I know are not from God. The Bible tells us what to do when those thoughts pop up: "We demolish arguments and every pretension that sets itself up against the knowledge of God, and *we take captive every thought* to make it obedient to Christ" (2 Corinthians 10:5 NIV).

How do we take our thoughts captive? First, by recognizing where negative thoughts come from—the devil. Second, by talking to God at that moment and asking him to redirect your thoughts. Another good thing to do is quote a scripture you have memorized or open the Bible and find a scripture that sets your mind in a better direction. The verse below is a great place to start.

> Brothers and sisters, think about the things that are good and worthy of praise. Think about the things that are true and honorable and right and pure and beautiful and respected. (Philippians 4:8)

EPIC RIDE

World Vision

World Vision is a Christian relief and development organization that helps poor children and communities in about one hundred countries around the world. They offer food and water during international emergencies, such as the earthquake in Haiti; they help children who have been orphaned by the HIV/AIDS crisis around the world; and they rescue children who are forced into the global sex trade or forced to fight in wars.

One of the best ways to get involved with World Vision is by sponsoring a child for $35 a month. I've supported a child for years, and I'm working with World Vision to let people know about the organization and about the huge needs that are out there. For more information on World Vision, visit www.world vision.org.

Extreme Christianity

Surfing is an extreme sport. It can be
dangerous, especially in huge waves, but it is a
thrilling experience. There are tons of other extreme
sports too, such as snowboarding, rock climbing, and
motocross.

Believe it or not, Christianity is extreme. Lots
of people in the Bible were extreme in their quest
to follow God, doing radical things in the name
of faith (think Paul, Moses, and Jesus). One of the
most extreme was Daniel. He risked his life for the
convictions and purpose God gave him. First, as a
young captive in Babylon, he obeyed God but defied
the king by refusing to eat the royal food that God had
asked his people not to eat. God spared his life when it
easily could have been taken. As an old man, he defied
a law that said no one could pray to anyone but the
Babylonian king, or they would be put to death. Daniel
prayed to God anyway and ended up being thrown
in a den of hungry lions. But because Daniel obeyed
God, God saved him by closing the mouths of the lions.
That's extreme—Daniel risked his life out of obedience
to God.

I want to be as extreme in my love and devotion for
Jesus as I am on my surfboard. I want to follow God
wherever he leads and do whatever he asks me to do
because I trust him—whether it's talking about him on
national television or being faithful to pray and spend

time with him every day. I want to obey God no matter what the price.

> My God sent his angel, and he shut the mouths of the lions. They have not hurt me, because I was found innocent in his sight. Nor have I ever done any wrong before you, O King. (Daniel 6:22)

Water of Life

I know water. I know about waves and surf and undertow and current and reef. My friends say I have salt water in my veins. But the water I surf in and the water I drink every day aren't enough.

The Bible has a great story about water. One day Jesus stopped at a well at midday. He talked to a Samaritan woman who was drawing water there. Jews never talked to Samaritans, and Jewish men would never talk to a Samaritan woman in those days, so what Jesus did was extreme. He told the woman that the water she was drawing would never quench the thirst she had in her soul. He said that only he could quench that thirst and that his Living Water would never run dry. The woman, whose life was desperate and full of sin, accepted Jesus' message. She'd still have to draw water every day to quench her physical thirst, but her spiritual thirst for God was quenched forever thanks to Jesus. Her life was changed eternally.

Are you filled with spiritual water or just physical water? If you don't have a relationship with God, your soul is thirsty for spiritual water; Jesus is the answer. Trust me. The water I surf in off the coast of Kauai, Hawaii, is beautiful and warm, but Jesus is the best Water ever. Trust him.

Jesus answered, "Everyone who drinks this water will be thirsty again, but whoever drinks the water I give will never be thirsty. The water I give will become a spring of water gushing up inside that person, giving eternal life." (John 4:13–14)

Master of the Impossible

Most people, including me, thought I'd never be able to surf again. I'd just lost my arm in a shark attack, and two arms seem pretty necessary to surf, period—let alone eventually compete as a professional surfer. Clearly we were wrong. God gave me the courage and passion to get back on the board only a month after the attack, and I'm competing regularly to this day.

Surfing again seemed impossible at first, but obviously God had other ideas. I believe that God did the impossible for me. In fact, he does impossible things every day. He heals brokenhearted people, forgives and changes the vilest sinners, and uses seemingly tiny events to bring people to himself. He heals people with illnesses, helps victims forgive those who hurt them, and helps enemies become friends. Better than all that, he saves us from the consequences of our sins. Lots of things seem impossible to us humans, but with God even those huge things are possible.

> Jesus answered, "The things impossible for people are possible for God." (Luke 18:27)

Women I Admire: Ruth

Ruth is one of the most well-known women in the Old Testament. She was a woman from Moab who decided to go with her mother-in-law, Naomi, to Naomi's home in Israel. Naomi's husband and sons had died in Moab, leaving both her and Ruth widows.

I admire Ruth because she decided that following God was important to her. She gave up everything out of love for her mother-in-law and for God. She faithfully served Naomi by working hard in Boaz's fields, gathering grain to make bread so they could survive. And God rewarded her for her faithfulness and loving heart. She ended up marrying Boaz, having a son, and becoming an ancestor of Christ.

I pray that I am willing to give up whatever it takes to follow God. And I pray that I can pass on a heritage of faith to my children, grandchildren, and great-grandchildren.

> But Ruth replied, "Don't urge me to leave you or to turn back from you. Where you go I will go, and where you stay I will stay. Your people will be my people and your God my God." (Ruth 1:16)

God Makes Us Different

So maybe my body is a little different than most of yours. The missing arm thing tends to throw people off at times, and some even stare at me. Sometimes I don't know if they're staring at me because they recognize me or because I'm missing an arm. Kids ask me questions or make weird comments about it too. Guess what? Just because I look different doesn't mean I'm bad or ugly. And just because your body looks different from other girls doesn't mean it's bad either.

God made each of us unique. God planned each one of us. He organized our bodies to be just what he wanted them to be, whether drop-dead gorgeous or a little plain, whether toothpick thin or a little chunky. When we complain about our bodies, we're really complaining about God's body. I'm not saying that we should eat whatever junk food we want, ignore exercise, have unhealthy habits, and then say, "This is the body God gave me."

I'm saying to appreciate the body God gave you, do your best to take care of it, and thank him for his good gifts.

> For you created my inmost being; you knit me together in my mother's womb. I praise you because I am fearfully and wonderfully made; your works are wonderful, I know that full well. (Psalm 139:13–14)

PRAYER

Dear Lord,

I thank you for this day. I pray that you would continue to use me to be a good witness to my friends and to be a light to them and to the world for you. Make your light shine through me brightly today in everything I do. And provide opportunities for me to show your love to others.

"You should be a light for other people. Live so that they will see the good things you do and will praise your Father in heaven." (Matthew 5:16)

JOURNAL OF
A SOUL SURFER

If you look around, you'll see chances to shine your light at your school, in your family, or even to people you don't know. Who in your life could use God's light right now? How can you make your light shine for them? Pray about it!

....

....

....

....

....

....

....

....

....

Eating Disorders

Eating too much? Not getting enough exercise? Eating too little? Exercising way too much? None of these are the way to go. Ballerina Sarah Lane struggled with weight, always wanting to be what she thought ballerinas should be: long and lean. Then she learned that a healthy weight is what she needs. Anorexia (not eating enough) and bulimia (eating then throwing up) can seriously affect your health and even kill you. Get help right away! God loves you too much for you to hurt your body like this. I encourage you to seek help first from God's Word and then from your family and friends or someone you trust.

If you're concerned with your weight or health, talk with your parents about consulting with a holistic health practitioner or clinical nutritionist who can help you come up with a nutritious eating plan that's right for you!

One Big Adventure

Life is a pretty big adventure when you're a surfer. There's the ocean, for one thing. The ocean is full of big waves and sharp reefs, currents and sea creatures. Then there arc wipeouts that can send you to the beach, sick rides on huge waves, and competitions around the world.

A life dedicated to following God is even more of an adventure. Ask Jonah, who ended up in the belly of a whale before helping a whole city repent and turn to God. Paul's life was pretty wild, what with all the travel, shipwrecks, jail time, and beatings. Think about Mary, Jesus' mother. One day she's just another engaged girl; the next day she's carrying God's Son. Each one chose the adventure of following God because each knew that God would provide the strength to do what he asked—even if they thought it was more than they could handle.

God gives you the strength too. He promises to help you do whatever he asks, just as he helped Jonah and Paul and Mary. Are you going to be a bored believer or an adventurous follower of God? More commitment + more depth = more adventure.

> I can do all things through Christ, because he gives me strength. (Philippians 4:13)

EPIC RIDE

Top Form

Being competitive in any activity takes lots of work. Whether you're surfing or playing chess or learning to drive, it's all about practice. That same determination is found in the Christian life. Salvation is a one-time event, but putting your salvation into practice takes work. Here are a few keys to success that apply to athletics and to your spiritual life:

1. Keep your priorities right. God and family first.
2. Work hard at what you want to achieve. If you want to be a competitive runner, you need to run. If you want to have a vibrant prayer life, you need to pray.
3. Spend time with people who encourage and help you. You can't expect to grow spiritually if you hang with the party crowd, just like you can't expect to become a great chef if you never hang out with people who cook.

Compassion in Action

It's always been in my heart to reach out and care for people in need, and since the attack I've been able to help in some pretty unique ways. I've visited and talked to a lot of children and adults who have lost limbs or had other injuries from accidents or fighting in a war. It seems to comfort people when they can meet someone else with a situation similar to their own. I've been able to donate time and money to organizations such as World Vision or to people who need it. I visited Thailand, one of the countries hit by the 2004 tsunami, to help orphaned children overcome their fear of the ocean that took the lives of their families and friends. These opportunities are so rewarding. They are a great way to give back to God the love and compassion he has given me.

God was a great comfort to me after the attack, and he continues to comfort me every day. He also tells us to comfort others when they need it. Sometimes even the littlest things make a big difference. Many times it's just a simple smile or a friendly hello to a newcomer at church that can change someone's life.

Make a difference! God comforts us; we are to comfort others. God has compassion for us; we are to have compassion for others. God helps us; we are to help others. Putting those words into action takes sacrifice, I know. But every day holds opportunities to reach out and show compassion to someone who

needs to see God's love. Give some of your own time to someone who needs to see God's love today.

> He comforts us every time we have trouble, so when others have trouble, we can comfort them with the same comfort God gives us. (2 Corinthians 1:4)

Sticking with the Jesus Recipe

Changing the recipe ruins the creation.
Try making your favorite cookie recipe, but leave out the flour, putting in baking powder instead. Replace the vanilla with Tabasco sauce. Put in salt instead of sugar. One bite and those cookies are in the trash.

It's the same with Christianity. You can't replace some of it with the teachings of other religions. Christianity is Christianity, and that's that. You can't take out the death of Jesus on the cross, or the fact that Jesus was God, and get the same Christianity. What you get is something God hates—lies.

God says we mustn't move away from the good news of Jesus' death, burial, and resurrection for our salvation. Like my mom always reminds me, the Word of God is historically and scientifically accurate, mathematically perfect, and confirmed by archaeology. Don't think for a minute that you can take what you like from other religions and still think you're following God. Stick with God and his Word only.

> But now God has made you his friends again. He did this through Christ's death in the body so that he might bring you into God's presence as people who are holy, with no wrong, and with nothing of which God can judge you guilty.

This will happen if you continue strong and sure in your faith. You must not be moved away from the hope brought to you by the Good News that you heard. (Colossians 1:22–23)

Weighing In

Weight seems to be a huge issue with us girls. Lots of girls struggle with wanting to be thin, which can lead to eating disorders such as anorexia or bulimia. I naturally want to look good. But looking good and obsessing are two different things.

I maintain a healthy weight by understanding that God wants me to take care of my body by making sure I eat healthy foods and exercise. I also know that God sees me as beautiful no matter what I look like. This is pretty reassuring because, with one arm, I look a little different than most people.

God wants you to be healthy physically, but more importantly, he wants you to be healthy spiritually. What's most important is your heart, not your hips. If you're not eating enough or are eating too much, confess those problems to Jesus and ask him for help. The same for your spiritual life. You can trust him. If you need to, seek out a youth group leader or a pastor who follows Jesus and lives by God's Word. Get on your way to a healthy lifestyle both spiritually and physically.

> Charm is deceptive, and beauty is fleeting; but a woman who fears the Lord is to be praised. (Proverbs 31:30)

Gossip

Do you gossip? Don't. It offends God and affects people's lives in a negative way. The Bible says in Proverbs 25:18 that gossip is like a sword or sharp arrow. It is dangerous. Don't be the one who shoots the arrow. Instead of gossiping, pray for the person, and keep what you heard or saw to yourself and God.

If you get caught in a conversation that leads to gossip, what can you do?

- Change the subject
- Leave as soon as possible.
- Encourage your friends to pray for the person instead of entertaining the gossip.
- Guard your mouth from participating in the gossip.
- Pray for yourself and your friends who are struggling with gossip.

The Big Spider (or Centipede or Lizard)

I live on the island of Kauai in the state of Hawaii. The plants, flowers, and wildlife are beautiful, but there are huge spiders and centipedes everywhere. I'm afraid of the poisonous spiders because they can hurt you. But I don't live my life in a state of paranoia or let my fear of them ruin my day. Fear can do that. It can make you act strange and stop you from enjoying the things around you, such as the beautiful flower the scary spider is resting on.

Just like these physical fears can stop you from experiencing what's around you, so spiritual fear can stop you from growing closer to God. Are you afraid all your friends will desert you if you become a Christian? Are you afraid God will send you as a missionary to someplace full of disease and danger? Are you afraid that if you dedicate yourself to God, he's going to test you with some terrible illness?

We all have fears, and it's not always a bad thing. But if you let fear get in the way of your trust in the Lord, it can destroy your life. Chances are, those spiders and centipedes aren't going to hurt you, and neither are your fears. They're just fears, nothing else. And God defeats fear every time. You can let your fear dominate and ruin all the good things in your life, or

you can rest in the peace and protection of God. You choose.

> For God has not given us a spirit of fear, but of power and of love and of a sound mind. (2 Timothy 1:7 NKJV)

> "I leave you peace; my peace I give you. I do not give it to you as the world does. So don't let your hearts be troubled or afraid." (John 14:27)

Listen Up!

My brothers and I love to listen to Christian music. We love the music of P.O.D., Project 86, Olivia the Band, Hillsong, and Bethany Dillon. They catch our attention not only because they're musically solid, but because the words honor God. Many secular songs are fun to listen to, but the words rarely honor God. God tells us to think about things that are good and worthy of praise and that are true, honorable, and pure (Philippians 4:8). He says this for a reason: he doesn't want us to be thinking about things that will not matter in the end.

Because music is such a big part of my life, I made a decision not to listen to music that will trash my mind with words and thoughts that aren't of God.

Do you listen to music that glorifies God? Pay attention to the words of the music you like, and then base your choices on what the Bible says.

> Let us come before him with thanksgiving and extol him with music and song. (Psalm 95:2)

Packing Your Bags

Imagine carrying three suitcases, two garment bags, a backpack, a briefcase, and two purses to school or work or church. It would be like me trying to surf wearing snowboarding gear, heavy boots, and gloves—what a burden! That's what it feels like when you carry guilt, hurt, bitterness, and unforgiveness in your heart.

Fortunately, God can take those burdens away from you. So instead of being buried in baggage, you can rest in the joy and peace he gives. But it means surrender and forgiveness. When I lost my arm, I could have been bitter toward God for what happened. But I made a decision to deny those feelings and instead enjoy the peace and joy God offers. You need to give up whatever is burdening you or, if there is nothing right now, decide in your heart to give it up before it even happens, like I did.

It may seem like you're being weak by admitting your pain, but it's exactly the opposite. God promises his strength to carry you, plus an abundant life, peace, and joy despite sorrow and pain. So drop those bags and stand up straight in God's freedom.

> "Come to me, all of you who are tired and have heavy loads, and I will give you rest. . . . The burden that I ask you to accept is easy; the load I give you to carry is light." (Matthew 11:28, 30)

PRAYER

God,

I pray that you will help me not to be influenced by this world but to keep my focus on you. Fill up my life with the truth of your Word, and let me see right through any lies that the devil might try to throw my way. May my eyes not turn to the right or to the left but be set directly on you.

"Then you will know the truth, and the truth will make you free." (John 8:32)

JOURNAL OF A SOUL SURFER

The world tries to get your focus off of God by getting you to believe its lies about beauty, popularity, and sin. What lies do you need to ignore? List them, and then find a Bible verse that tells you the truth about that situation. Write a prayer to God asking for his truth to be your focus.

....

....

....

....

....

....

....

....

Women I Admire: Mary

Mary, Jesus' mother, was a strong young woman who had a solid relationship with God. She served God with her whole heart. Because of that, he chose her to birth his Son. She knew she'd face ridicule when her family, friends, and townspeople found out she was pregnant. In fact, they could have stoned her if her fiancé agreed to it. She knew Joseph might doubt her story, perhaps thinking she'd cheated on him.

Instead of running from God, demanding that he not choose her, Mary humbly agreed to give birth to the Son of God. She recognized her role in God's plan, and despite the stares and gossip and trouble she would have to face, she clung to the promises God had given her. In fact, she rejoiced that God honored her with his Son and praised his name.

I admire Mary because she humbly did what God asked her to do regardless of what anyone thought. I hope that you, too, will draw near to God, recognize his call on your life, then do whatever he asks in submission to his great plan.

> Then Mary said, "My soul praises the Lord; my heart rejoices in God my savior, because he has shown his concern for his humble servant girl. From now on, all people will say that I am blessed, because the Powerful One has done great things for me. His name is holy." (Luke 1:46–49)

The Real You

One of the things people asked as I
recovered from the shark attack was whether I was
going to get a good prosthetic arm. It sort of seemed
like a good idea, and a company offered to make me
one. So I had one fitted and made to look like my real
arm. It looks very natural, but it doesn't function on
its own. It just hangs off my shoulder. I've worn it a few
times but found that for an active person like me, it just
gets in the way. Although prosthetic arms are great for
some people, the fake arm just isn't my thing. So now
the arm hangs on the back of my bedroom door. My
brothers and I use it to play jokes on people.

Are there things in your life that don't fit? Things
that get in the way of what God created you to be? Get
rid of those things. Instead, seek God, and he will bring
you the things that fit you best.

> Each one of us has a body with many parts, and these
> parts all have different uses. In the same way, we are
> many, but in Christ we are all one body. Each one is a part
> of that body, and each part belongs to all the other parts.
> (Romans 12:4–5)

Sunscreen

I'm in the water all the time, and water reflects the sun. If I'm not careful, I could get sunburned. Doctors are always saying that too much sun damages the skin and can lead to scary things like skin cancer. So I use a strong, natural sunscreen to block those ultra-violet rays. For those of you who live in winter zones, winter sun can do just as much damage, and the cold air dries and chaps skin. Also, if you ski or snowboard in the mountains, the higher you are above sea level, the worse the ultraviolet rays. So use a sunscreen with a high SPF, and apply it often.

Just as we need to protect our skin from damage, we need to protect our hearts from damage. God's Word is the ultimate "sin-screen." Hiding God's Word in your heart and living by it will protect you from the damage of sin.

Standing Strong

I've heard the story of a young Christian named Danae. One day some popular kids at her small Christian school asked her if she wanted to try a cigarette. She said, "No, thanks," but then said that she'd tried cigarettes before but wasn't in the mood right then. She wanted to impress them but ended up telling a lie. She had never tried cigarettes and had no intention of doing so.

Maybe you're afraid to stand up for what's right. Somebody asks if you want a beer, and you say, "Not now." Maybe somebody starts telling a story about another girl in the youth group. Instead of saying, "Stop it," you walk away, saying you need more cookies.

Stand by your convictions! God wants you to. He set that example for us through Jesus. Live by God's standards, because how you respond to those little temptations will make a big difference in your life and heart (and in other people's lives too). Don't be afraid to let others know what your standards are—and then live by them. God will bless you for your honesty and faithfulness.

> Be alert. Continue strong in the faith. Have courage, and be strong. (1 Corinthians 16:13)

A Taste of the Bible Every Day

In December 2003 I made a commitment to read the Bible every day. I don't have a set time or place, so I may read late at night or early in the morning before heading out to my favorite surfing spot. It could be one verse or one chapter, Old Testament or New Testament.

I realize that it's important to fill my mind and heart with the words of God. I've taken to heart that verse in Psalm 119 that calls God's Word a "lamp" and a "light." The Bible is a great guide for everyday life as I deal with friends and family and people I don't know at all, and it helps illuminate God's plan for my life. It helps me figure out what's important, what my priorities should be, and how I should act.

In a world where everybody has an opinion about how you should live your life, it's nice to have something that never changes and is filled with truth and wisdom for day-to-day life. The Bible is also clear about what it means to be a Christian and have a relationship with the living God. If you have questions about becoming a Christian, read the Bible.

You can also check out the devotion titled "Salvation" on page 89. God wants to get to know you and wants you to get to know him. Bibles are easy to come by for most of us these days. So pick one up and

get into a serious relationship with our loving Father through reading his Word and praying.

> Your word is a lamp to my feet and a light for my path. (Psalm 119:105)

Favorite Bible Verses

- When you need a daily reminder of how to start your day . . .

  Finally, be strong in the Lord and in his great power. Put on the full armor of God so that you can fight against the devil's evil tricks. (Ephesians 6:10–11. Continue reading verses 12–17 too.)

- When you want to encourage someone to persevere . . .

  When people are tempted and still continue strong, they should be happy. After they have proved their faith, God will reward them with life forever. God promised this to all those who love him. (James 1:12)

- When you're thankful . . .

  Sing to the Lord a new song; sing to the Lord, all the earth. Sing to the Lord, praise his name; proclaim his salvation day after day. Declare his glory among the nations, his marvelous deeds among all peoples. (Psalm 96:1–3)

- When you need a dose of courage . . .

  Have I not commanded you? Be strong and courageous. Do not be terrified; do not be discouraged, for the LORD your God will be with you wherever you go. (Joshua 1:9)

  For God has not given us a spirit of fear, but of power and of love and of a sound mind. (2 Timothy 1:7 NKJV)

- When you're tempted . . .

  The only temptation that has come to you is that which everyone has. But you can trust God, who will not permit you to be tempted more than you can stand. But when you are tempted, he will also give you a way to escape so that you will be able to stand it. (1 Corinthians 10:13)

- When you're angry . . .

  Do not be bitter or angry or mad. Never shout angrily or say things to hurt others. Never do anything evil. Be kind and loving to each other, and forgive each other just as God forgave you in Christ. (Ephesians 4:31–32)

- When you just want to give up . . .

  Always be joyful. Pray continually, and give thanks whatever happens. That is what God wants for you. (1 Thessalonians 5:16–18)

- When you're making an important decision . . .

  I guide you in the way of wisdom and lead you along straight paths. (Proverbs 4:11)

  Trust in the LORD with all your heart and lean not on your own understanding; in all your ways acknowledge him, and he will make your paths straight. (Proverbs 3:5–6)

Popularity Contest

Everybody wants to be liked by people,
to fit in, to be part of a group. Sometimes, however, it
isn't that easy to find a group you fit in with. While I
fit in with my surfing and church friends and with my
surfing team, I maybe wouldn't fit in so easily at an
East Coast prep school or a southern country club.

It doesn't matter. As Christians we're all part of
one big family, whether you're from Grand Rapids,
Michigan, or Paris, France. There is no "in" group as
children of God. How we look or how much money we
have or what sport we participate in doesn't matter to
God. What matters to God is our hearts and if we are
his children.

This is reassuring, because we all struggle to
find our place, especially as teenagers. Whether it's
at school or church, having a group of friends seems
important. But with God as our Father and fellow
believers as our brothers and sisters, we're all family
and should treat each other lovingly and equally—the
way our Father taught us.

If you have a close group of friends, don't forget
to reach out to others! And if you don't have that close
group of friends, it's okay; be friends with everyone!

> But to all who did accept him and believe in him he gave
> the right to become children of God. (John 1:12)

Bad Dates

First of all, you do not need to date. Period. Save your heart for your husband! Don't date until you know you're ready to marry. For now, enjoy your friends. If you like someone, it's best to hang out in groups and get to know him as he interacts with others. Find a good youth group to do activities with, and just be friends.

I'm not a dating expert, but I've witnessed some pretty bad experiences through people I know. I don't want any of you to be stuck in a bad situation with a guy, and neither does our Father, God. So be smart if you are thinking about dating. Do your research before getting into any relationship with a guy.

- Does the guy have a relationship with God? Does he have a prayer life and spend time in God's Word?
- Does he have a respectable reputation?
- What is his lifestyle like? What do his family and friends say about it?
- What kinds of people does he choose to hang out with? Do they encourage him to do unholy things?

- Does he have goals for the future? Are the goals respectable ones?
- Does he have integrity?

Ask these questions about yourself while you're at it!

These are all things that you should consider before getting into any relationship. I recommend waiting for God to bring someone into your life who has all the qualities you are looking for and who will be a good influence and companion. For now, focus on honoring God in all that you do. He knows how to treat you right, love you, care for you, and fulfill your every need.

Living for Christ in the World

School dances and post-football game parties can be fun. But what do you do when the dancing becomes vulgar or when a guy who likes to use girls asks you to dance? What do you do when beer is served at a party, or when people start making out, or when someone offers you drugs?

This is a test of your obedience to God. If you've committed to living for him, you've made a decision that involves self-sacrifice—denying yourself from doing something you know is wrong no matter how much you want to do it. Although giving in once may seem minor, it actually makes it harder for you to say no in the future. There is no need to feel the pressure to give in to these situations. God knows it's hard, and he always provides a way out (1 Corinthians 10:13).

You have many options to help you make the right decision in dangerous situations at a party or group event: (1) you can decide not to go in the first place, (2) you can attend with a group of Christian friends who have the same values you do and will back you up on your convictions, and (3) you can take a stand and say no to immoral behavior. The important thing is not to sacrifice your testimony for Christ just to fit in with people. Either avoid places where temptations are

plenty or arm yourself with God's Word. Stand up for what you believe is right!

Everything you do or say should be done to obey Jesus your Lord. And in all you do, give thanks to God the Father through Jesus. (Colossians 3:17)

Talk the Talk

What do you like to talk about every day?
Do you talk about your favorite band? Your new clothes? Your last surf session? God? "Yeah right," you say. "I can't talk about God. People will think I am nuts." Maybe so, but if you love God as much as you say, you'll talk about him.

When I started getting asked to do interviews, I saw it as a great opportunity to give God the credit for everything he did in my life. He worked so many miracles the day I was attacked and in the weeks that followed. He deserves the glory for them all. I try to talk about him with everyone I meet, whether it's with the media or my neighbor next door. I love God so much, and I want to talk about him as much as possible and share the love and peace he has given me.

I encourage you to let Christ shine through you in everything you do. The Bible says, "You should be a light for other people. Live so that they will see the good things you do and will praise your Father in heaven" (Matthew 5:16).

> So through Jesus let us always offer to God our sacrifice of praise, coming from lips that speak his name. Do not forget to do good to others, and share with them, because such sacrifices please God. (Hebrews 13:15–16)

EPIC RIDE

Waiting Until Marriage

The pressure to have sex is huge. Sex has become so casual in our culture. What is the big deal about having or not having sex before marriage? The big deal is that God created sex for a purpose—to unite a man and a woman in marriage. It's important to God that we use the things he created for the purpose he intended. I've committed to wait until marriage before having sex. If you haven't waited for marriage and you feel guilty because of what you did, know that God offers forgiveness and a chance to start over and become a virgin again in his sight. Ask God for forgiveness today, and stay pure for your future husband.

> You should know that your body is a temple for the Holy Spirit who is in you. You have received the Holy Spirit from God. So you do not belong to yourselves, because you were bought by God for a price. So honor God with your bodies. (1 Corinthians 6:19–20)

Finding the Positives

God wants us to focus on having a good attitude, even when bad things happen. It's easy to focus on the negatives instead of the positives. When I fall off my board, my negative thoughts say, *I blew it!* My positive thoughts say, *I can do better next time,* and I paddle back out and find another wave. It's so easy for me to focus on what I can't do because of only having one arm. Instead, I daily make a point to focus on the blessings God has given me—like the fact that I still have one arm!

Consider your own thoughts. Does the devil try to bring you down with negative thoughts about yourself or your situation? Don't let those thoughts linger in your mind. If you do, they will consume your thinking. Concentrate on God's goodness, and challenge yourself to overcome whatever you're struggling with. God can help. When negative thoughts sabotage your heart and mind, they turn into lies. Don't ever believe them. Believe in what God tells you about yourself. God loves you and always will. Meditate on this scripture and promise from the almighty God: "The LORD appeared to us in the past saying: 'I have loved you with an everlasting love; I have drawn you with loving-kindness'" (Jeremiah 31:3).

> Brothers and sisters, think about the things that are good and worthy of praise. Think about the things that are true and honorable and right and pure and beautiful and respected. (Philippians 4:8)

Practicing Patience

I get a little impatient at times. I want
bigger and better waves right now, or I want my mom
and dad to hurry up. But God calls us to be patient
with others, to be patient in seeing God's plan for our
lives, and even to be patient with suffering and pain.

Where do you struggle when it comes to patience?
Are you impatient with people who don't understand a
math concept as quickly as you do? Do you get frustrated
when the line is really long at the theme park? Do you
rant and rave about physical limitations? Maybe you're
impatient when it comes to waiting for God's plan to
happen for you. Impatience shows itself in many ways.

When you notice yourself getting impatient, make
an effort to improve in that area. Ask God for patience
as you struggle, and remember that learning patience
takes patience. Use those moments to thank God for his
blessings, to pray for someone, or to memorize Scripture.
Practicing patience is a challenge you'll have for the rest
of your life—we all do!

But God can help you as you learn, and during the
process you'll start bearing the fruit of patience. You'll be a
blessing to those around you and a light for Jesus as well.

But the Spirit produces the fruit of love, joy, peace, patience,
kindness, goodness, faithfulness, gentleness, self-control.
There is no law that says these things are wrong. (Galatians
5:22–23)

Women I Admire: Sarah Hill

Sarah Hill is a great friend to me and to my family. She was one of the first people at the hospital after I got attacked by the shark. She drove my brother Noah to the hospital, calming and comforting him despite her own fear.

Sarah is a youth counselor and several years older than me, but she is one of my closest friends. She challenges me to be strong when I am weak-hearted, prays for me, and uplifts me when I need encouragement. I encourage and pray for her too. She's always giving to others, offering support and love for my friends and me, even when she has a lot going on in her own life. It is important to have friends like Sarah who will mentor and disciple you biblically and help you grow closer to God.

I pray that I will have a willing servant's heart like Sarah and find joy in helping and loving others. I hope, too, that you will find someone like that in your own life and allow God to speak to you through that person. You could even be a friend like that for someone else.

As iron sharpens iron, so one man sharpens another. (Proverbs 27:17)

Dear God,

I pray that you will help my friends to grow stronger in you. I thank you so much for the good friends you have given me. Allow me to see the needs my friends have and how you can fill those needs through me. Help me to show my friends that I love them all the time.

A friend loves at all times. (Proverbs 17:17)

JOURNAL OF
A SOUL SURFER

Being a great friend takes effort. What are some specific ways that you can be more loving to your circle of friends? What about ideas on building friendships with those outside your circle?

....

....

....

....

....

....

....

....

....

....

Thanks for Everything

Some of you might think it is hard to be thankful for a shark taking my arm. But I am. I'm thankful because I know God directs my life and has a plan for me. He is using me to tell others about him in ways I never could have imagined before the attack. I'm also thankful that I can experience the sunrise as I begin my day surfing, thankful for the lush flowers and plants that grow on Kauai, my home. I'm thankful for my family and friends and for how God is teaching me so many spiritual lessons. I'm also thankful I don't have to worry about the next steps of my life, because God is working it all out.

So even though there are rough times and hassles, fatigue, and lots of time away from home, I'm thankful for what God has given me and what he's doing with my life. The Bible says to give thanks to God in all circumstances. How can we thank God when something bad happens? We can thank God by remembering that he loves us and that everything that happens in life—good and bad—is working toward the completion of his overall plan.

> Give thanks to the LORD, for he is good. His love endures forever. (Psalm 136:1)

WIPEOUT

Wipe Out Your Pride

Surfing involves a lot of focus, balance, and control. If you lose focus, get off balance, or lose control of your board, you'll wipe out. One minute you're riding; the next you're underwater. Life can be very much the same way. Downfalls can happen instantly, and all of a sudden you're crying for help.

In Proverbs 16:18 it says, "Pride goes before destruction, a haughty spirit before a fall." I can get so caught up in thinking I'm doing great that pride starts to seep into my heart. I use this verse to keep my heart in check so I don't get prideful. It's a good one to memorize.

Training for the Big Event

I do a lot of training for big surfing competitions. I work on balance, do lots of aerobic exercise, and practice like crazy. Other athletes train as well. Runners, skiers, skaters, gymnasts, hockey players, weight lifters, and swimmers all train for big events. That training takes hard work and lots of perseverance. It pays off, though, when you accomplish the athletic goals you set for yourself.

Christians also train for the race Jesus calls us to—the race called life. There are a couple of things to remember when training for Jesus' race. First, keep your heart strong. Just as runners and surfers need to be in shape aerobically, so we need to be in shape spiritually. We spiritually shape up through prayer, reading God's Word, having faith, and acting on it.

Also, keep your goal in mind. It's pointless to train with no goal. Our spiritual goal is the approval of Jesus—which means avoiding laziness, complacency, and a bad attitude. Finally, keep the prize in mind. For Christians, it's eternity with God and a special place in his kingdom—a prize well worth the hard work we put into training and living a life for him.

> You know that in a race all the runners run, but only one gets the prize. So run to win! (1 Corinthians 9:24)

God Never Leaves

I've been in some scary situations. The minutes and hours after the shark attack were frightening. I was afraid on the long paddle into shore, afraid as I waited for the ambulance to arrive. There were also times when I had to speak in front of people or talk to people who were famous. But although fear was a part of those experiences, a bigger part was knowing that God is always with me.

A powerful thing was said to me as the ambulance pulled out of the parking lot that Halloween day in 2003 with its sirens blaring. The paramedic leaned over and whispered in my ear, "God will never leave you or forsake you." He was so right. I've learned a lot about God since the attack, but one of the main things is that he is always with me. He's always with you too. Whatever, whenever, wherever. God is always by your side.

> The Lord himself goes before you and will be with you; he will never leave you nor forsake you. Do not be afraid; do not be discouraged. (Deuteronomy 31:8)

God Created Diversity

I surf with people from many different countries and many different ethnic backgrounds. I've also visited a number of different countries. One thing I've noticed is that people—no matter what they look like, where they live, or how smart or athletic they are—are just people.

God loves every one of us. Singer tobyMac talks about diversity among God's children in his *Welcome to Diverse City* album. He talks about how, no matter what we look like, we're all part of God's big body. That's so true.

I'm a surfer, but I can't understand algebra without help. Maybe you can't sing but really like to cook. God created us all with different gifts and abilities for a purpose—to be a part of the body of Christ. Enjoy your gifts, and bless others with them. That's how God designed us to be, and it's great!

> If each part of the body were the same part, there would be no body. But truly God put all the parts, each one of them, in the body as he wanted them. So then there are many parts, but only one body. (1 Corinthians 12:18–20)

Everybody Needs a Friend

Do you have a group of friends you always hang out with? It's only natural to gravitate toward certain people. But don't let that stop you from talking and hanging out with people who don't quite fit in with your friends because of looks or different interests. God calls us to love everybody, not just people like ourselves. He asks us to treat everyone with respect no matter how old, young, rich, poor, ugly, beautiful, mean, or nice they may be. It's important to treat everyone the way Jesus would treat them.

Maybe you don't have a friend right now, or maybe you're new to an area. Focus on your friendship with God, and reach out to others as he would.

God loves everyone and commands us to love them too. I urge you to love everyone with the love Jesus shows to you.

> This royal law is found in the Scriptures: "Love your neighbor as you love yourself." If you obey this law, you are doing right. But if you treat one person as being more important than another, you are sinning. You are guilty of breaking God's law. (James 2:8–9)

Die to Self

"I'm not pretty." "My hair is ugly." "I'm too fat." "I'm different from everyone else." Ever say things like this to yourself? You may tell yourself you're ugly or fat or weird, but God doesn't focus on those things. In his eyes you are his beautiful daughter—created for a purpose and loved with an undying love.

It's destructive to talk yourself into believing you're worthless. In fact, it's selfish. If I spent all my time telling myself I'm ugly or different because I'm missing a limb, I'd miss what God was trying to do through me. When it's all about me, it's not about God. "Jesus said to all of them, 'If people want to follow me, they must give up the things they want. They must be willing to give up their lives daily to follow me'" (Luke 9:23).

Meditating on scriptures can be useful to stop selfish thoughts. Some wonderful scriptures to meditate on are found in Jeremiah and John: "I have loved you with an everlasting love; I have drawn you with loving-kindness" (Jeremiah 31:3). "The Father himself loves you" (John 16:27).

> The LORD is righteous in all his ways and loving toward all he has made. The LORD is near to all who call on him, to all who call on him in truth. (Psalm 145:17–18)

Women I Admire:
Joni Eareckson Tada

Joni Eareckson Tada was a teenager
when she dove into the water and broke her neck.
In that split second, she became a quadriplegic. But
she didn't let that tragedy stop her from following
God. In fact, Joni has had a huge impact around the
world through her unwavering testimony about God's
goodness.

Joni has written many books, recorded music,
created stunning works of art, and has her own radio
program. In 1979, she founded Joni and Friends,
whose goal is to share the gospel and equip churches
worldwide to evangelize and disciple people with
disabilities.

Joni has traveled the world in her wheelchair and
hasn't let her disability stop her from sharing the news
of Jesus and encouraging others with disabilities. If
you have a disability, don't let it stop you from serving
God. Remember, he has a very specific purpose for your
life. No one else can do what he wants to do through
you. So use what you have to spread the news of God's
love—and that goes for all of us!

> But he said to me, "My grace is enough for you.
> When you are weak, my power is made perfect in you."
> (2 Corinthians 12:9)

Helping Others:
Here Are Some Ideas

1. Read a book to an elderly person who has poor eyesight.
2. Volunteer with your church youth group, or help with the children's ministry.
3. Mentor a younger student who is having trouble in math, science, or reading.
4. Volunteer at a soup kitchen or food pantry throughout the year (not just during the holidays!).
5. Volunteer to babysit for a single mother or a mom who is home all day with several youngsters.
6. Offer to teach an older person how to do simple computer tasks such as using e-mail, the Internet, or a word-processing program.
7. Go on a mission trip with your church.
8. Pick up trash at the beach or a park.
9. Mow the lawn, shovel snow, or plant flowers for an older person.
10. Make dinner for your family, and give your mom the night off.

Whom Are You Living For?

Everyone wants to be liked. We want to have friends and fit in with a group. The problem comes when we try so hard to please people and make them be our friends that we forget who we are.

Jesus knew all along that his only job was to please his Father in heaven. He didn't try to please the church leaders of his day. He also didn't try to please his disciples or the crowds who heard him speak. He didn't live to become famous or to hear nice words from people who liked him. Jesus' one goal on earth was to please God by fulfilling the purpose he was made for—to show us how to live, and to die on the cross for our sins (John 3:16).

What is your goal in life? Is it to please God? What if you started living to make God happy and fulfill the purpose you were created for (Jeremiah 29:11)? Your life might be a lot different than it is now. You'd worry less about what other people think. You'd care a lot less about having treasures on earth and a lot more about doing what God created you to do. Seek God's purpose for your life today.

> I was put to death on the cross with Christ, and I do not live anymore—it is Christ who lives in me. I still live in my body, but I live by faith in the Son of God who loved me and gave himself to save me. (Galatians 2:20)

Log in the Eye

As humans, we tend to be judgmental of the people around us. You might hear about someone who just got arrested and say, "What a sinner" or "What a bad person! I would never do that." We get so caught up in judging the actions of other people and trying to fix their problems that we overlook our own hearts and our own problems.

The Bible says it's like noticing a speck of dust in your friend's eye but not seeing the wood plank sticking out of your own eye. Jesus tells us that this is hypocritical: "First, take the wood out of your own eye. Then you will see clearly to take the dust out of your friend's eye" (Luke 6:42).

This is a parable, of course, but it reminds us to focus on getting our own hearts in line with Jesus' heart before we even concern ourselves with other people's problems. Realize that you do have sin in your life. Don't overlook it. Let the Holy Spirit deal with it right now.

> "Why do you notice the little piece of dust in your friend's eye, but you don't notice the big piece of wood in your own eye?" (Luke 6:41)

The Rock and the Hard Place

Jacob, the son of Isaac and grandson of Abraham, had traveled through the desert, alone and exhausted, until he fell asleep with a rock for a pillow. While he was napping, he had a dream in which God told him that he would be with him, watch over him, and never leave him. Jacob woke up reassured of God's presence and God's direction for his life.

I've felt God's presence throughout my life, and I've sensed his presence from the moment the shark took my arm. God promised that he would never leave me or forsake me (Deuteronomy 31:6). So I knew he was with me on the paddle, at the hospital, during rehabilitation, and when I got back on the board for the first time. I know God is with me to this day as I surf, compete, and travel around the world. God is by my side every second of the day and night, just like he promised.

According to God's promise, I can have courage when I'm up against fear because my God who loves me is there by my side. Just as God promised Jacob he'd always be with him, he promised you the same thing. In good times and bad, God will never abandon you.

> I am with you and will watch over you wherever you go, and I will bring you back to this land. I will not leave you until I have done what I have promised you. (Genesis 28:15)

Employment Opportunity

We all have different jobs at various times in life. Your job may be babysitting, working at a restaurant, or just going to school and studying. Mine may be pro surfing, or it may be working as a nutritionist someday.

But it turns out we all work together because we have the same employer: Jesus. Everyone who believes in Jesus has the privilege of telling others about him. There is a story in the Bible about the apostle Paul. Paul urged his younger friend Timothy to preach the news of Jesus and be ready to tell others what they needed to do to follow God. He urges us to do the same thing.

What's cool is that you can work for Jesus at the same time you're doing other jobs. This is accomplished by being a good example and acting the way Jesus would act. Whatever the circumstances and wherever you are, Jesus provides opportunities for you to do what he called you to do. Tell others about him.

Preach the Good News. Be ready at all times, and tell people what they need to do. Tell them when they are wrong. Encourage them with great patience and careful teaching. (2 Timothy 4:2)

Lord,

I pray that you would keep me safe today and watch over me. Be to me what you were to King David in the Bible: a protector and friend. Help me to be observant of the way you work so I can be more like you.

Be my rock of refuge, a strong fortress to save me. (Psalm 31:2)

JOURNAL OF
A SOUL SURFER

The world can be a scary place sometimes. Make a list of things you fear, little and big. Then pray for God's protection, and hand those fears over to a much bigger God.

....

....

....

....

....

....

....

....

....

....

The Big Lie

What really matters in life? Happiness? Power? Wealth? Those are things our culture has told us are important. Those are things we are told we should aim to achieve. But Jesus wants you to think about the future—*What good is all that stuff after I die?* The Bible teaches that our souls live on past our physical death. And if you believe that Jesus is God's Son and live by faith in him, your soul will enter into heaven to be with the loving Creator for eternity. Because of this, Jesus told us to store up our treasures in heaven—not on earth, where they can be destroyed, stolen, or lost.

To store up treasures in heaven, you constantly have to set your eyes on the spiritual things you cannot see. This would include introducing people to God's Word, encouraging new Christians, showing love to others, and having compassion for the hurting. When we humbly do those things (and more), it's like storing up treasures in heaven—with results we can enjoy forever!

I try to base all my decisions on my love for Jesus and my eternal future with him. So set your sights on God and his unseen plans.

We set our eyes not on what we see but on what we cannot see. What we see will last only a short time, but what we cannot see will last forever. (2 Corinthians 4:18)

Bad Decisions

Watching your friends make bad decisions is heartbreaking. You can't prevent them from making decisions that damage their bodies, reputations, and faith, but you can encourage them to make the right decisions:

1. Pray for them. Ask God to protect them and convict them of the wrong they're doing.
2. Confront them. When you see your friends hurting themselves or others, talk openly to them about it. Don't yell, get mad, or ridicule. Point out the truth in love.
3. Love them. Your friends need you. They may not say it, but knowing they have a loving and steady friend who is always there is a big help.
4. Be a good example for them. Don't let yourself get caught up in making bad choices too.

My people are destroyed from lack of knowledge. (Hosea 4:6)

The Right Path

If you've ever read or listened to *Pilgrim's Progress* by John Bunyan, you'll know that Christian had to choose between the narrow, difficult path to heaven and the path that seemed wide and easy but led to hell. In reality, we are given the same option. We can choose the path of sin or the one that leads to eternity with God.

Christian chose the narrow path. It was strenuous and hard, but it led to Jesus. That's the key—being led. Here's an analogy: Say you are lost in the jungle and are looking for a particular village. Then you stumble across a trail and think to yourself, *This might be the way to the village. But even if it's not, it will take me somewhere, so I'll try it.* Just then, a villager pops out of the bushes and says he knows the way to the village you are looking for. He instructs you to follow him, not the trail. You are hesitant at first because there is no trail the way he came. The villager says, "Trust me. This is the way, my father is the chief." Here are your options: you can take the trail alone, or you can be led by the chief's son.

So which way are you choosing to go? Know that you can trust Jesus. His way is right. He will lead you into eternity with the Father in heaven.

> He restores my soul. He guides me in paths of
> righteousness for his name's sake. (Psalm 23:3)

EPIC RIDE

True Friendship

There's a great example of true friendship in the Old Testament. David, a shepherd boy who killed Goliath and became a great leader of Israel, found a true friend in Jonathan, son of King Saul. Jonathan protected David from Saul's anger, saving David's life more than once. David mourned when they had to part, and he mourned when Jonathan died. Their friendship lasted through very tough times, even death. Then David took care of Jonathan's descendants as well.

Here are a couple of things to learn about friendship from David and Jonathan:

1. A friend always protects. Jonathan protected David's life many times. You can protect your friend's reputation.
2. A friend does what's right. Jonathan knew it was wrong to kill David, despite Saul's command, so he spared David's life. Do what is best for your friend.
3. A friend loves at all times. It would have been easy for Jonathan to turn on David, but he didn't. You can love your friend despite the opinions of others.
4. A friend is loyal. David was so loyal to Jonathan that he protected Jonathan's descendants. You won't turn on your friend even when others do.

Peace Meets Storm

Tough times are inevitable. We have all faced tough days or even weeks and months, and if you haven't, you will. Sometimes it's an illness, or someone you love dies, or maybe it's a family problem such as divorce or an unplanned pregnancy. My family and I have had some tough times, including when I was attacked by a shark and lost my arm and when my grandfather died. The amazing thing is that God promises his children peace right in the middle of tough times.

One day Jesus and his disciples were crossing the Sea of Galilee in the northern part of Israel. As often happens in this region, an afternoon storm came up. The disciples were scared as the winds and rains lashed at their boat. Jesus, however, was sound asleep. When he woke up, he took one look at the storm and said, "Quiet!" The storm stopped immediately.

Just as Jesus brought peace to the waters of the Sea of Galilee, he can bring peace to you in the midst of troubles. He may not make the troubles go away, but he will bring peace to your heart. When the shark attacked, God immediately gave me peace in the middle of the turmoil that was going on in my mind and heart during that traumatizing experience (Philippians 4:7). Ask him for peace in your situation.

> Jesus stood up and commanded the wind and said to the waves, "Quiet! Be still!" Then the wind stopped, and it became completely calm. (Mark 4:39)

Feeding on God's Word

Have you ever stuffed yourself so full you
thought you'd puke? Ever scarfed down enough candy
to sink a ship? Guzzled enough Coke to float? We feed
our bodies all the time, but often what we put in isn't
healthy. Although junk food will keep us from starving,
it won't help our bodies grow stronger and stay healthy.
It's not enough.

It's similar in our spiritual lives. God wants us to feed
our spiritual selves on the Word of God. He doesn't want
us eating spiritual junk food. What's spiritual junk food?
How about reading all kinds of Christian books but
never reading the Bible? Attending lots of conferences
and workshops but never lifting a finger to help at your
church or in your neighborhood. Listening to Christian
music without listening to Christ himself.

We need to grow stronger spiritually. Start
nourishing your spirit by studying the Bible on your
own and putting what you learn into action. Then those
extra things (watching Christian movies and listening
to Christian music) become even more enjoyable and
applicable to your life.

> Your words came to me, and I listened carefully to them.
> Your words made me very happy, because I am called by
> your name, LORD God All-Powerful. (Jeremiah 15:16 NCV)

It's All About Timing

Jesus knew he would be King one day.
The Jewish people thought he would take over Israel, be their king, and free them from Roman rule. But Jesus knew his Kingship wasn't about ruling a nation on earth; he knew he would rule in a spiritual realm. When the people wanted to make him king, he said no. He was living according to God's timing and not the world's.

God has an appointed time for everything. My family and I had hoped I would rise through the surfing ranks, establish a career in surfing, and bring the light of Jesus to the surfing industry. But October 31, 2003, was God's appointed time to change the course of my life. As you know, that was the day of the shark attack.

I always knew I wanted God to use me however he could, but I never expected it to be like this! God's timing is perfect according to his plan, and I'm learning to live according to his timing. The great thing is that I have established a career in surfing, and I *am* able to do the things we had all hoped for, even with one arm. He's got more plans for me that will happen when the timing is right. He has plans for you too. The only thing we have to do is wait for him to work everything out. In the meantime, follow him.

For what has been determined must take place. (Daniel 11:36)

WIPEOUT

The Results of Sin

King David experienced the results of sin after he caught sight of Bathsheba bathing on her roof. It all started with a lustful look. Then he seduced her, a married woman, and got her pregnant. One lie led to the next until he conspired to have her husband killed.

But when David was confronted about these sins, he begged God's forgiveness. God forgave him, but David had to live with the consequences of his actions. (Read about it in 2 Samuel 11 and 12.)

If you are caught in sin right now, please know that God will forgive you no matter what you've done. But also know that you and the people around you will live with the results of your sin. You aren't loved any less by God, and he'll use your past for his glory.

Broken for God

Did you know that shepherds will
sometimes break the leg of a sheep that constantly
wanders away? The sheep is then forced to stay close
to the shepherd for protection—and because it hurts
to walk on that leg. It seems cruel, but the shepherd is
trying to protect the sheep from ending up alone, lost,
and at risk of being lunch to a hungry wolf.

God is our Shepherd. He takes care of us, protects
us, and leads us toward rest and restoration. When we
wander away, he brings us back.

Maybe you keep wandering away from God and
heading toward danger. The Good Shepherd is going to
come after you because he loves you and doesn't want
you to get hurt. You have the choice to return to him or
continue to walk away. He will bring you back to himself,
possibly broken, but hopefully with him for good. Don't
ever doubt his love. Trust him. He is the Good Shepherd.
He cares for you and will never give up on you.

> The Lord is my shepherd, I shall not be in want. He makes
> me lie down in green pastures, he leads me beside quiet
> waters, he restores my soul. He guides me in paths of
> righteousness for his name's sake. Even though I walk
> through the valley of the shadow of death, I will fear no
> evil, for you are with me; your rod and your staff, they
> comfort me. . . . Surely goodness and love will follow me
> all the days of my life, and I will dwell in the house of the
> Lord forever. (Psalm 23:1–4, 6)

Photos by Noah Hamilton, noahhamiltonphoto.com

Surfing is a beautiful lifestyle.

Above: I love getting barreled, but a big air is just as rewarding.
Below: A Tahitian sunset after a long, fun surf session.

Photo by Noah Hamilton, noahhamiltonphoto.com

Doing a cutback while surfing in a NSSA competition in Kona, Hawaii, at age 13, about six months before the shark attack (April 2003).

Photo by Noah Hamilton, noahhamiltonphoto.com

My very first competition with one
arm in January 2004, two months after
the shark attack. I placed fifth and got the
motivation I needed to keep competing!

Photo by Noah Hamilton, noahhamiltonphoto.com

Me and Mom in the hospital recovery room, surrounded by so many beautiful flowers and balloons—gifts from our friends in the community.

This mock-up surfboard was used in my movie, *Soul Surfer*. It's a close replica of my actual board, clearly showing the shark bite.

Above: I like to pray with my dad, or another family member, before I go out in my contest heats. We pray for waves, my competitors, and God's will.

Opposite page: In the movie, this cross sits in front of the beach-tent church my family attends. Interesting fact: the director came to my real-life church and another friend's church on our island, and he based the movie church on some of the elements he liked from them!

Photos by Noah Hamilton, noahhamiltonphoto.com

Above: An image from Tahiti while shooting for my movie, *Soul Surfer.* This was an amazing ride—only a surfer knows the feeling.

Opposite page, top: One of the better barrels of my life. This was on a boat trip through the Mentawai Islands with my family.

Opposite page, bottom: Here's a cool point of view . . . do you feel like you're in the barrel with me?

This underwater photo is of me duck diving. The formation of the wave can be so beautiful from below!

Photo by Noah Hamilton, noahhamiltonphoto.com

Me, during a portrait session for *Soul Surfer* the movie.

Photos by Noah Hamilton, noahhamiltonphoto.com

Above: NSSA Nationals 2005—this is one of the turns that helped me win my first national title!

Opposite page: My *ohana,* which means "family" in Hawaiian. From left to right: Becky and Noah, Tim and Hana (the dog), Mom and Dad (Cheri and Tom), then me! My oldest brother, Noah, married Becky in May 2009.

In the movie, "Bethany" goes on a World Vision mission trip. In this particular scene, you will see me (during my cameo) in the background of the shot.

On the set in "Bethany's room" with *Soul Surfer* director, Sean McNamara, I got to take a peak through the lens and see what they were shooting—so cool!

A great portrait that my brother Noah took of me.

PRAYER

God,

Right now as I sit down to read your Word, I pray that you will help me to understand it better and apply it to my everyday life. Teach me something about yourself that I never knew before. And guide me through your truth so I can follow in your footsteps.

Your word is a lamp to my feet and a light for my path. (Psalm 119:105)

JOURNAL OF
A SOUL SURFER

The Bible is like God's big guidebook on how to live your life.
What questions would you like answers for right now? Make a
list, pray for direction, and then get out your guidebook.

....

....

....

....

....

....

....

....

....

Women I Admire: Cheri Hamilton

My mom went through a lot growing up.
She came to Hawaii when she was about twenty years old so she could surf. There she met my dad, got married, settled down, became a Christian, and had three children. They taught my two brothers and me to surf when we were little.

My mom taught me more than just surfing, though. She taught me about God, introducing me to him when I was very young. She showed me God's love in so many ways, and she shows God's love to others as well. My mom is also a prayer warrior. She prays all the time, teaching me about the power of prayer. We pray together about everything. We pray about surfing competitions, we ask God to speak through me and calm my nerves before I go to a speaking event, and we pray that he would use me in whatever way he wants to.

I thank God for my mom and the example she's been to me through the years. I pray for her every day, and I encourage you to pray for and with your mom or another adult who is important to you.

> Pray continually, and give thanks whatever happens.
> That is what God wants for you in Christ Jesus.
> (1 Thessalonians 5:17–18)

A New Role

Pretend you land a small role in the school play. You have one line and get to walk across the stage once. Then the director calls you in and says you now get to take the lead role, with lots of lines and a lot of time on stage. All of a sudden you have a new script to learn and a new character to become.

Becoming a Christian is sort of like landing a new role. Before you accepted Jesus, you talked and acted a certain way. With Jesus in your life, you are asked to talk and act completely different. You leave the old role behind and take on a new one.

God instructs us to replace bad language and gossip with words of encouragement and love; to no longer act selfishly, but to think of others as being more important than ourselves. In doing this, our goals change from only pleasing ourselves to considering mission work or just living life to help people. It's a whole new role Jesus has given us. And it's a leading role in his kingdom!

> If anyone belongs to Christ, there is a new creation.
> The old things have gone; everything is made new!
> (2 Corinthians 5:17)

EPIC RIDE

A List of Thanks

What are you thankful for? Instead of droning on about how bad your life is, come up with a list of what you are thankful for. The list might include the following:

1. Your family. Sure, they may be weird, but they're yours and you love them.
2. Your education. Many girls around the world receive little or no education. Be thankful for the opportunities you have.
3. Your home. You may have a tiny house with crummy furniture and have to share a room with your sister, but you do have a house. Many people around the world live in dirty shacks or on the street.
4. God's protection. God protects his children from evil. This doesn't mean everything in your life is great, but it does mean God knows what's going on.
5. God's mercy. We all deserve to die for our sins, but God provided for us through the death of his Son.
6. Salvation. Look at what we have to look forward to . . . eternity in the presence of God's love.

Salvation

Nothing is better than personally knowing Jesus. God created everything for a purpose—including your life! He desires to have a personal relationship with you. It's hard to believe that the Creator desires to personally know you and me, isn't it?

The Bible tells us that all have sinned and fall short of God's glory (Romans 3:23). Our sin keeps us from knowing God's will for our lives. God knew that we would not live perfect lives, but he loves us anyway. And to help us, God sent Jesus, his Son, to die for our sins. Romans 5:8 says, "But God shows his great love for us in this way: Christ died for us while we were still sinners."

I love that the Lord loves us just the way we are. The only thing for us to do is admit that we need Jesus. "Ask, and God will give to you. Search, and you will find. Knock, and the door will open for you. Yes, everyone who asks will receive. Everyone who searches will find. And everyone who knocks will have the door opened" (Matthew 7:7–8).

If you realize that you want to receive forgiveness and have God enter your life, I encourage you to pray (talk to God) and tell him everything. Tell him you realize you are a sinner and are sorry for your sin. Tell him you want to experience his love and find truth. Start your relationship with him today.

I'd love to hear about how you came to Christ. E-mail me through my website at www.bethanyhamilton.com.

Sticking Up for Your Friends

I try to stick up for my friends. If I hear someone talking negatively about one of them, I encourage them to stop. It is good to talk about how great your friends are, how honest and smart and talented they are, and how much you appreciate them. I really appreciated the way my friends came to visit me in the hospital after the attack.

The apostle Paul also stuck up for his friend. In his letter to Philemon in the New Testament, Paul asks Philemon, a Christian, to forgive Onesimus, a slave who stole from Philemon, then ran away. Onesimus ended up in Rome, where he met Paul and became a Christian. Paul grew to love Onesimus but knew he must return to his master to ask for forgiveness and return what he stole. That's why Paul wrote the letter.

What an honor it is to stick up for your friends.

> I, Paul, an old man now and also a prisoner for Christ Jesus, am pleading with you for my child Onesimus, who became my child while I was in prison. . . . I am sending him back to you, and with him I am sending my own heart. (Philemon 9–12)

Epic Waves and Troughs

Surfing is about riding the face of the waves, about letting the power of the wave propel you along its line toward shore. Every wave is different: there are big waves, small waves, barreling waves, sloping waves, "sectiony" waves, and the list goes on. The ride is always different too. Between the waves are the troughs, the low parts that can't be ridden, which means a lot of waiting and sometimes getting pounded by other waves. Sometimes it seems as if there are numerous troughs to get through before riding a really good wave.

Life is like that too. It would be great to always be riding the wave, always experiencing its power; it is like being on a spiritual high all the time. But along with the times of epic spiritual waves, there are times of trudging through the spiritual troughs of life. Lots of spiritual growth happens in those troughs, and lots of day-to-day living too. It's a good time to read your Bible, pray, hang out with Christian friends, and get involved in a Bible study. Whatever you do, stay strong, whether you're riding the epic spiritual wave or barely making it through the spiritual trough. Remember that God loves you no matter which place you find yourself in today.

So my dear brothers and sisters, stand strong. Do not let anything move you. Always give yourselves fully to the work of the Lord, because you know that your work in the Lord is never wasted. (1 Corinthians 15:58)

God Looks at the Heart

I'm so glad God cares about what's going on inside me. He cares about my heart: my attitudes, my salvation, and my insecurities.

Samuel learned this about God when God sent him to anoint his choice as the new king of Israel. Seven of Jesse's sons came before Samuel, all of them looking like good king material. Each one was strong, tall, and handsome. But God told Samuel that his chosen king was not any one of them. So Samuel asked if Jesse had any more sons. Jesse summoned his youngest boy, David, from the fields. Then God said, "This is the one; anoint him." God knew that David was "a man after his own heart" (1 Samuel 13:14). Samuel experienced God looking at the heart, not the outward appearance.

It's reassuring that God doesn't choose people based on looks. He only looks at our hearts.

> But the Lord said to Samuel, "Do not consider his appearance or his height, for I have rejected him. The Lord does not look at the things people look at. Man looks at the outward appearance, but the Lord looks at the heart." (1 Samuel 16:7)

What's a Boyfriend Anyway?

I notice nowadays that the age girls start having boyfriends is getting younger and younger. And I think people are rushing in to relationships too young. No girl needs a guy to feel loved. For now let's enjoy the love of our family, friends, and God. God loves us so much that we don't need to look for love in a guy.

Not that guys are bad. I have plenty of guy friends who are fun to hang out with at church. And I love my brothers and my dad. It's just that our culture tells us girls that having a boyfriend will make us happy. Magazines are full of articles about how to attract a guy, keep a guy, dress for a guy, and kiss a guy. Television and movies also make it seem that every girl has a boyfriend. Wrong. No girl needs a boyfriend to make her feel complete. That is God's job.

If you are looking for happiness in a guy, you won't find it. Happiness comes from God. Is it a good idea to be looking for love in the wrong places? No way.

The Lord your God is with you, he is mighty to save. He will take great delight in you, he will quiet you with his love, he will rejoice over you with singing. (Zephaniah 3:17)

The Best Advice

What do you do when you have to make a decision? Let's say you have to decide whether to go on a summer mission trip or stay home and work. You probably talk it over with your friends to see if any of them are going on the trip or to see what they think of the idea. You talk about it with your parents to see if you can afford the trip and if they will let you go. Maybe you talk to your youth leader to see if she thinks you're spiritually ready.

But do you pray? James 1:5 tells us to ask God for the wisdom we need. What a great plan! When I'm faced with a decision, such as which surfing competition to attend, how to spend money, or when and where to travel, I talk to my parents, but I also pray first. God is the greatest One to ask because he's the wisest.

God's answers usually aren't broadcast over the Christian radio station or written in the sky. His answers are quietly heard through prayer, opportunity, or other people. First you ask; then you listen for the answer.

> But if any of you needs wisdom, you should ask God for it. He is generous to everyone and will give you wisdom without criticizing you. (James 1:5)

Selfishness

The *New American Heritage Dictionary* defines the word *selfish* as "concerned chiefly or only with oneself, without regard for the well-being of others." What that means in real life is that a selfish person thinks only about herself. She makes only herself happy, makes herself look good all the time, and makes sure she doesn't have to do anything she doesn't want to do.

Selfish is the opposite of what God calls us to be. James 3:14–15 says, "But if you are selfish and have bitter jealousy in your hearts, do not brag. Your bragging is a lie that hides the truth. That kind of 'wisdom' does not come from God but from the world. It is not spiritual; it is from the devil."

The man answered, "Love the Lord your God with all your heart, all your soul, all your strength, and all your mind." Also, "Love your neighbor as you love yourself." (Luke 10:27)

Resisting Temptation

It's no surprise that temptation is hard
to face and overcome. After all, it's been around since
Adam and Eve. King David fell to the temptation of a
pretty woman. Jesus' disciples were tempted, and even
Jesus was tempted. They all fell except Jesus, because
he's God.

You can overcome temptation through prayer,
knowledge of God's Word, and common sense. Prayer
prepares you to fight temptation and enlists God's
help. But God also gives each of us a brain. If you're
tempted to shoplift, stay out of the stores. If you're
tempted to drink, don't go to parties where there is
beer. If you're tempted to mouth off to your mom, leave
the room first. If you're tempted to go too far sexually,
don't be alone with your boyfriend. These are kind of
"Duh!" things, but sometimes we don't think.

You know temptation is going to come. First, pray
and ask God for help; then depend on God to help you.
Second, stay away from that temptation in the first
place. God and common sense. What a concept!

> God is strong and can help you not to fall. He can bring you
> before his glory without any wrong in you and can give you
> great joy. (Jude 24)

Women I Admire: Gladys Aylward

Most people would have lost heart when told they had flunked out of missionary training school, but not Gladys Aylward. Instead, she saved enough money working as a maid to buy a train ticket to China, then embarked on the long, dangerous journey. She reached China, introduced herself to a longtime missionary, and made her home in Yangcheng for nearly twenty years.

After rough times of persecution, Gladys was eventually accepted into the Chinese culture because of her true desire to befriend the people and share Christ's love. She started an orphanage and led many people to Christ. When the Japanese invaded China, she led almost one hundred children to safety on a long journey over the mountains despite her own fear and exhaustion.

I admire Gladys Aylward because she knew where God had called her and she let nothing stop her. She worked tirelessly for God, often in dangerous places, with no concern for her own safety. She was faithful and fearless, two things I pray that I can be for God.

Even though I walk through the valley of the shadow of death, I will fear no evil, for you are with me; your rod and your staff, they comfort me. (Psalm 23:4)

PRAYER

Dear Lord,

I pray that you would help me to be nicer to my parents and to obey them when they ask me to do something. Continually remind me that you gave them that role in my life for a reason and that by respecting and obeying them, I am pleasing you. Thank you for my parents. I love you.

Children, obey your parents in all things, because this pleases the Lord. (Colossians 3:20)

JOURNAL OF A SOUL SURFER

God knows that having a strong relationship with your parents will bless you today and in the future. What can you do this week to show kindness and respect to your mom or dad?

....

....

....

....

....

....

....

....

....

EPIC RIDE

My Salvation Experience

Nobody made me believe in God or get saved. Sure, my parents brought me to church, and we prayed and talked about God at home, but the decision to accept Christ as my Savior was mine. I remember putting my trust in Christ when I was about five years old. Some people might think I was too young, but I know that I have a personal relationship with a living God and that Christ means everything to me. You can never be too young to come to Jesus. Jesus himself said, "Let the little children come to me. Don't stop them, because the kingdom of heaven belongs to people who are like these children" (Matthew 19:14).

Promoting Peace

A girl wrote me recently on my message board saying that school is awful because people make fun of her friends' braces, call people names, and play pranks on the new kids. All this was at a Christian school!

God calls us to be peacemakers, to promote peace wherever we are. He tells us not to participate, encourage, or allow something that would make someone look or feel stupid. This means not making fun of people, not teasing, and certainly not bullying. It also means standing up for those who are being teased or bullied. It a choice we all must make: doing what's right in God's eyes or looking cool in a bully's eyes. What will you choose?

> Deceit is in the hearts of those who plot evil, but joy for those who promote peace. (Proverbs 12:20)

Free to Be Me

My job is not to make everybody happy.
If it were, I'd be flying all over the country to speak, doing interviews, and never having time to surf. It's also not my job to make myself happy. If it were, I would be surfing all the time and never taking time to do books like this one or tell other people about Jesus.

I'm so glad I don't have to please anyone but God. God brings opportunities into my life that he wants me to follow. He brings people into my life who he wants me to meet. I just need to do what he asks, and that's a pretty freeing feeling.

It feels good that I don't have to be the boss of my life. Are you the boss of your life? I hope not, because the Bible says we need to please God, not ourselves. This means you *not* trying to control everyone around you, you *not* having to be the center of attention all the time, and you *not* having to worry about what will happen in the future. After all, you're *not* the boss. Your job is to work for the Boss, doing only what he asks you to do.

"I don't try to please myself, but I try to please the One who sent me." (John 5:30)

The Way of the World

The Bible talks about not loving the things in this world, but what does that really mean? Loving the things of the world means loving popularity and money and wanting only the best things (clothes, car, money, etc.). It means following the rest of the world and allowing others to dictate where you stand on different issues. Sometimes I am shocked by what people do just because others are doing it. When you live as the world does, you are often blinded to the truth. I see so many people who lose themselves just so that they can be like others.

It is hard to be a strong Christian all the time—especially when it means going against what some of your friends are doing. I have found that the only way I am able to be a Christian who is walking boldly with Christ is to daily depend on God for my strength. It doesn't mean that I have to dress ugly, behave weirdly, or not have any fun (believe me, I have a lot of fun!). It simply means that I have different priorities, and daily I make a choice to follow the Lord. A Christian's priorities include God, family, fellowship, standing up for what is right, and keeping yourself pure from sexual sin. Reading the Bible is a great way to help you make the right choices; it is the way to remain strong as a Christian.

God doesn't want us to try to do it on our own; we just need to ask him. So ask him!

Do not love the world or the things in the world. If you love the world, the love of the Father is not in you. These are the ways of the world: wanting to please our sinful selves, wanting the sinful things we see, and being too proud of what we have. None of these come from the Father, but all of them come from the world. (1 John 2:15–16)

Parents Need Forgiveness Too

Several of you wrote on my message board about dealing with your parents. It's a hard issue, that's for sure, and I don't have all the answers. In fact, I only have three small answers that God gave us in the Bible: obey, forgive, and pray. First, the Bible says to obey your parents. Generally they know what's best for you. (It's another story if your parents ask you to do something illegal or immoral. That's when you go to another adult you trust.) I try to do what my parents ask because the Bible says to, and they usually know more about what's best.

The second answer is forgiveness. Parents do things wrong too. They can snap at you, ignore you, or put too much responsibility on you. If you can, talk to your parents about these things; then forgive them. And I don't mean only if they ask you. Forgive them anyway because God asks you to, and then love them. After all, God loves you when *you* mess up. He loves your parents too. If you're having serious trouble with your parents, please talk to your youth pastor, school counselor, a teacher or an adult you trust, and—most importantly—God.

The third answer is to pray. Praying for your parents is probably the best thing you could do for them. When you pray, it allows God to do amazing

things in people's lives. He alone can work miracles. Your parents need prayer as much as the rest of us, so put them in God's hands every day.

> Bear with each other, and forgive each other. If someone does wrong to you, forgive that person because the Lord forgave you. . . . Children, obey your parents in all things, because this pleases the Lord. (Colossians 3:13, 20)

Divorce

The Bible mentions divorce many times. Jesus talked about divorce in Matthew 19, and Paul talked about it in 1 Corinthians. Neither of them liked divorce, but both recognized that divorce happens. You shouldn't hate your parents if they are divorced; you really need to forgive them. And being the child of divorced parents doesn't make you any less of a Christian. Your obligation is to love your parents and obey them. It's also to love God and obey him. Remember that God loves you, no matter what your parents do.

A Friend to All

Here's what one visitor said on my message board: "I think having close friendships with other Christians is so important because we need to encourage each other and hold each other accountable in our everyday life as well as in our relationships with Jesus Christ. I believe it is equally important to be a good friend to those who don't know God and not to shut them out. God came into the world to save sinners (all of us), and he would never turn from anyone, and I know he wants his followers to do the same."

I agree with her. It's hard to share the love of Jesus with others if the only people you know are Christians. It's also hard to grow in Jesus if all your friends are non-Christians. God calls us to balance our spiritual growth by befriending Christians and reaching out to those who aren't. Make sure your friendships are a mix of both. After all, Jesus became friends with sinners and changed their lives, but he also spent time with his twelve disciples. He had the perfect balance.

Jesus said to his followers, "Go everywhere in the world, and tell the Good News to everyone." (Mark 16:15)

Justice God's Way

Ever want to lash out at someone who says cruel things to you? Ever want to get back at someone who talks behind your back or spreads lies about you? Ever feel like hurting someone who has hurt you? Don't. Justice is God's job.

The first Christians were persecuted mercilessly. Jews who became followers of Christ were ostracized; later, Christians were hunted down and killed in cities all over the Roman world. Several of Christ's disciples were crucified. In fact, Christians are being persecuted right now all over the world. Some say that more Christians are being killed today than ever before.

It's easy to want to hurt people who hurt you or who hurt other Christians. Fortunately, punishing those wrongs isn't our job. It's God's. We may want people punished right away for the wrongs they have done, but God will bring about justice according to his plan. Don't worry: God will avenge the wrongs done to and against his people.

God calls us to love our enemies and pray for them. Matthew 5:43–45 says, "You have heard that it was said, 'Love your neighbor and hate your enemies.' But I say to you, love your enemies. Pray for those who hurt you. If you do this, you will be true children of your Father in heaven. He causes the sun to rise on good

people and on evil people, and he sends rain to those who do right and to those who do wrong."

My friends, do not try to punish others when they wrong you, but wait for God to punish them with his anger. It is written: "I will punish those who do wrong; I will repay them," says the Lord. (Romans 12:19)

EPIC RIDE

How to Make a Difference for God at School

The Bible talks about not loving the things of the world, but it's pretty hard to do that every day at school. Here are some ways you can make a difference for God at school.

1. Stand up for people who are being picked on.
2. Make friends with someone who doesn't have any friends.
3. Never cheat. Ever.
4. Avoid talking about someone behind her back.
5. Respect your teachers, the principal, and other adults.
6. Do your best work on tests and homework.
7. Show up to class on time, prepared, and ready to participate.
8. Talk about God when it's appropriate.
9. Dress modestly.
10. Never bully, tease, or play mean jokes on people.

Fragrance of the King

Several years ago I was offered the
opportunity to endorse a perfume line called Stoked
and Wired. Some of the proceeds of these fragrances
are being used to support people in need through
World Vision. World Vision is a Christian relief and
development organization dedicated to helping children
and their communities worldwide reach their full
potential by tackling the causes of poverty. Thinking
about these fragrances, I am reminded that God thinks
of us, his children, as perfumes. Weird, I know.

In the Bible he calls us "the sweet smell of Christ."
Just as the smell of perfume permeates the air, the
love of God should permeate others' lives through us.
We are the fragrance of God in the world. Although
it's great to know that the profits of Stoked and Wired
are being used by God to minister to kids around
the world, it's even better to know that my life is a
fragrance to be used by God. I pray that I will be a
sweet-smelling Christian who reminds people of God's
great love.

> But thanks be to God, who always leads us as captives
> in Christ's victory parade. God uses us to spread his
> knowledge everywhere like a sweet-smelling perfume. Our
> offering to God is this: We are the sweet smell of Christ
> among those who are being saved and among those who
> are being lost. (2 Corinthians 2:14–15)

PRAYER

Dear Lord,

I thank you so much for my wonderful family, for my awesome friends, and for all the blessings and gifts you've given me. Thank you even for the hard situations that are in my life right now. I know that you are in control, and don't ever let me forget that. You have a master plan, and all of these struggles and good times fit into that plan perfectly. So I am grateful for that. And I'm thankful that you are always right by my side and that you've given me such great friends and family. Thank you for loving me.

Let us come before him with thanksgiving. (Psalm 95:2)

JOURNAL OF
A SOUL SURFER

We can't see how all the good and the bad in our lives fit into God's big plan. Write down all the things you are (or should be) thankful for, even the tough situations. Then come back to that list in a few years to see how both the easy times and the hard times fit into his master plan for your life.

....

....

....

....

....

....

....

....

....

Slow to Anger!

Everybody gets angry. Parents get mad at each other and at their kids. Employees get mad at bosses. Teachers get mad at students. Friends get mad at each other. Sometimes I get mad at myself!

Jesus got angry when he saw the temple filled with merchants and money changers. He overturned tables and benches, driving out the people who had turned the temple into a marketplace. Jesus, however, did not sin. His was a righteous anger.

Sometimes I get angry when things don't go the way I plan or when I have a junk surfing session. I know that during these times I am living in the flesh. Other times I see people hurting or in need, and I get upset. I get angry when I see Christians who are not honoring God. God wants me to be moved by the things that move him. But he does not want me to waste time being an angry Christian.

Many times it is easy for us to get angry when we feel like we have been mistreated. I don't like feeling angry; it just makes me want to cry. If you are feeling angry today, and it is not for a righteous cause, take a moment to ask God to help you get rid of that anger. He is able to do that, and it will make you feel a lot better.

My dear brothers and sisters, always be willing to listen and slow to speak. Do not become angry easily, because anger will not help you live the right kind of life God wants. (James 1:19–20)

Women I Admire: Rachel Joy Scott

Rachel Scott was murdered on April 20, 1999, at Columbine High School. She was shot by her classmates, who had planned the killings for weeks. When the shooters asked Rachel if she believed in God, she proudly said yes. Those were her last words. At her admission of her love for God, she was shot point-blank and killed.

Rachel's life was not in vain. She wanted to be used by God, and through her death she was. One way her death was used by God is that her family and friends started Columbine Redemption, a nonprofit organization that includes "Rachel's Challenge," which trains young people to reach out to fellow students who are handicapped, neglected, new to school, or picked on by others. Rachel understood the importance of standing up for her faith in God no matter the cost, and now her family is helping other young people put those words into action.

Rachel stood up for God. She chose death rather than denying her love for God, and in death her love lives on. I pray I can be as strong as Rachel, and I pray that you can too. Today, may we say yes to Jesus and take a stand in our schools.

Jesus said to her, "I am the resurrection and the life.
Those who believe in me will have life even if they die.
And everyone who lives and believes in me will never die."
(John 11:25–26)

Making Adjustments

I've had to make some adjustments to my surfboard since losing my arm in the attack. My dad noticed I was having a hard time duck diving (pushing the surfboard under the breaking waves as I paddle out to where I'll surf). He saw a handle on the side of a lifeguard rescue board, and it inspired him to make something similar for me. He used two stick-on leash plugs, surgical tubing, and rope to put a strap on the front center of my board.

The strap helps me duck dive as well as pull myself up and center myself on the board while lying down. I'm probably the only surfer with a hand strap, but then again I'm probably one of the few surfers with one arm. That strap was a big adjustment but a very necessary one.

Sometimes I have to make adjustments in my walk with God to bring him back to the center of my life. You probably do too. You may have to turn off the computer or TV so you can spend more time reading the Bible, or you may have to make new friends because your current ones aren't helping your spiritual life. Take some time to figure out what adjustments you need to make in your life to put God first, and then ask God to help you make them. Like that hand strap, the adjustments are worth the effort. They'll help you get recentered in your relationship with God.

Jesus looked at them and said, "For people this is impossible, but for God all things are possible." (Mark 10:27)

Judging Your Neighbor

It is definitely a struggle not to judge the people around you, not to look at their actions or words and interpret them in a judgmental way. For example, you might see a girl from your church going into an abortion clinic. It would be easy to think she is pregnant and seeking an abortion. But maybe the girl is going to the clinic with an unsaved friend to help her tell the clinic she doesn't want an abortion after all.

Judging people only gets us in trouble. You might vow never to speak to the girl and tell others what you saw, which would only spread malicious gossip and hurt her. Instead, by giving her the benefit of the doubt and offering grace instead of judgment, you give God the chance to work in her life and yours.

Also, consider that you yourself don't want to be judged by others. God tells us that he is the only judge. He is the only One who knows each person's heart, so he is the only One who can judge that heart. Evaluate your heart. Are you judging other people? Don't try to do God's job. Instead, show love and forgiveness and mercy as he instructs us to do.

> "Why do you notice the little piece of dust in your friend's eye, but you don't notice the big piece of wood in your own eye?" (Matthew 7:3)

God is the only Lawmaker and Judge. He is the only One who can save and destroy. So it is not right for you to judge your neighbor. (James 4:12)

Smoke Not!

The University of Michigan's C. S. Mott Children's Hospital web-site (www.med.umich.edu/mott/) lists five reasons teens choose to smoke:

1. Peer pressure. You are trying to fit in.
2. Entertainment. It's fun to smoke at parties or with friends.
3. Curiosity. You want to see what it's like.
4. Rebellion. Your parents say no, so you say yes.
5. Stress. You think it will relax you.

Trying that first cigarette (or any other kind of drug) is more than just experimenting. It's a lifelong decision; because once you're hooked, it's very hard to quit. So before you experiment with cigarettes (or any other substance), ask yourself if you want to be an addict for your whole life. It's an ugly, smelly, unhealthy, dangerous, and expensive bad habit. Is that the kind of "cool" you want to be?

God's Timing Is Perfect

Some girls think that if they haven't developed certain curves by the time they're thirteen, they're never going to. Some think that they need a boyfriend by age fifteen or they will become social outcasts. Some girls even think that if they aren't married by twenty, they're going to be old maids. If you see yourself in these statements, you should know you're living in the Worldly Time Zone.

The world, the home of Satan himself, sets all sorts of standards based on random things. When we don't meet those standards, we think we are bad. Wrong. Having a boyfriend or the right shape or a wedding ring has nothing to do with what others are doing and everything to do with God's timing. God's timing is not our timing, but it's certainly perfect for each one of us and for his ultimate plan.

I know I want to live according to the God Time Zone. I pray for patience and understanding to help me wait for what God wants for me. After all, God's plans always happen. Those plans just happen in his time, not ours.

> For the revelation awaits an appointed time; it speaks of the end and will not prove false. Though it linger, wait for it; it will certainly come and will not delay. (Habakkuk 2:3)

First Love

Jesus was the first to truly love you the way no one else could. We go through periods of time when we really sense God's presence and love in our lives more than other times. Remember a time when you were really on fire for God? Think about how you felt—loved, excited, joyful, and eager to follow him.

Many times, however, those feelings fade. We get complacent and bored in our relationship with God. But it's reassuring to know that even when we don't feel anything, God still loves us and is right by our side. In Revelation, John talks about a vision he had in which Jesus asked him to write a letter to the church in Ephesus. The Ephesian believers had forgotten their first love—that amazing, profound, beautiful love and passion for God. John urges them to seek it again.

If you've lost that passion for Jesus, it's time to get back on track with him. He can reignite that love within you.

> "But I have this against you: You have left the love you had in the beginning. So remember where you were before you fell. Change your hearts and do what you did at first." (Revelation 2:4–5)

The Real You

Sometimes it's hard to tell where you
begin and your friends end. Do you feel like you're so
busy trying to fit in with your group of friends that
you've lost who you are? Consider these questions:

1. What do you do when you go to the mall with
    your friends and they want to shop for clothes
    but you want to go to the bookstore? Do you
    skip the books and head for the skirts or tell
    them you'll meet them in an hour at a specific
    store?
2. All your friends seem to act up in youth group.
    They talk, pass notes, and ignore the speaker,
    but you think it's better to pay attention and
    actually learn something. Do you do what your
    friends do or encourage them to be respectful?
3. You think having a boyfriend is stupid right
    now, but all your friends seem to have one. Do
    you find a boyfriend quickly, or do you enjoy
    your Friday nights without the pressure of
    having to be perfect for a guy?

God made you who you are. Are you willing to
ignore how God made you in order to fit in with other
people? I know I'd never give up surfing, going to
church, or sharing Jesus just so I could fit in with a

group. I hope you won't give up on the real you, the girl God created and made unique.

> I praise you because I am fearfully and wonderfully made; your works are wonderful, I know that full well. (Psalm 139:14)

True Friends

Friendship can be tough sometimes.
Some of my friendships have changed since the shark attack. Some people have become better friends; some have grown distant. I've made a lot of new friends as well. My true friends always stand by me, and I stand by them.

Here are some characteristics of true friends:

1. A true friend sticks by you through the bad times.
2. True friends forgive each other. It's not always easy to tolerate her bad moods or sharp words, but patience and forgiveness go a long way.
3. True friends tell the truth. It's hard to tell her that she's going too far with her boyfriend or that her eating habits (too much or too little) are dangerous, but a true friend will always be honest.
4. A true friend looks past the outside to what is inside. It's not clothes or hair or straight teeth that matter, but the heart.

What kind of friend are you? Now is a good time to be the kind of friend you'd like to have. Remember, too, that Jesus is the ultimate example of a friend. He loved us enough to die for us, after all (John 15:13).

A friend loves at all times, and a brother is born for adversity. (Proverbs 17:17)

EPIC RIDE

Did You Know? Bible Basics

- The Bible is the living Word of God.
- The Bible is made up of the Old Testament and the New Testament.
- The New Testament has 27 books; the Old Testament has 39.
- The first five books of the Old Testament are called the Pentateuch; the first four books of the New Testament are called the Gospels.
- John Wycliffe translated the Bible from Latin into English in the 1380s.
- The King James Version (KJV) of the Bible was completed in 1611.
- The complete New International Version (NIV) was finished in 1978.
- The ten plagues that God, through Moses, brought on the Egyptians were water turned to blood, frogs, gnats, flies, plague on the livestock, boils, hail, locusts, darkness, and death of the firstborn.
- Jesus told more than 50 parables in the New Testament.
- The Bible was written in three different languages: Hebrew, Aramaic, and Greek.
- The Bible is the best-selling book ever.

True Beauty

Regina Franklin wrote a book called *Who Calls Me Beautiful*? It's about how women and girls view their bodies and the struggles we face in this area. In the book she talks about what real beauty is and offers a surprising definition of God's opinion of true beauty. It's found in John 3:16 (see below).

Does that seem a little weird? It did at first to me too. But if you think about it, she's right. God defines beauty as salvation. He doesn't care if you're the most beautiful girl on the planet or the one with frizzy hair and a big nose. Acne? Big thighs? Stubby nails? Doesn't matter. God's idea of beauty is a person who believes in him and who accepts the gift of salvation. It's a spiritual issue, not a physical one.

What kind of beauty are you? A spiritual stunner in God's eyes or an outwardly beautiful girl with an ugly heart on the inside?

> God loved the world so much that he gave his one and only Son so that whoever believes in him may not be lost, but have eternal life. (John 3:16)

I Surrender All

Mary (not Jesus' mother) sacrificed a lot to pour perfume on Jesus' feet. In those days people saved for the future by investing in things such as expensive spices and perfumes or land. So it was a big thing for Mary to pour out that investment.

Jesus knew she was giving him her future, her plans, and her life. That perfume signified everything Mary had, and she humbly gave it to Jesus. Some of the disciples didn't understand. They figured she was wasting her resources or should have sold the perfume and given Jesus the money.

Maybe you've given up something lately for Christ. Have you decided that mission work instead of a high-paying job is how God wants you to live your life? It could be something as simple as giving up spring break on the beach to help at an orphanage in Haiti. Or giving up a bit of your reputation to stand up for the kid everybody picks on. Whatever sacrifice we make for Christ is so much better than what we keep for ourselves.

You may have friends or family who don't understand, just as the disciples didn't understand Mary. But Christ understands fully the sacrifices we make for him.

"This woman did the only thing she could do for me; she poured perfume on my body to prepare me for burial. I tell you the truth, wherever the Good News is preached in all the world, what this woman has done will be told, and people will remember her." (Mark 14:8–9)

Women I Admire: Jackie Pullinger

Jackie Pullinger's book *Chasing the Dragon* opened my eyes to the horror of drug abuse and the power of the love of Jesus. Jackie tells about being called by God to Hong Kong to work with the prostitutes and drug addicts living in the notorious Walled City. She was just twenty years old.

She prayed over them and told them about Jesus, but nothing changed. Then God showed Jackie that she needed to do more than pray with them; she needed to show them God's love by providing food, shelter, and health care to these people. Soon she saw God's power in action as addicts turned to Jesus and away from drugs. Even the Triads, secret criminal gangs, gained respect for her.

I pray that God would give me the courage to serve him wherever he calls me and the love to reach out to those who seem to be the most degraded, hopeless people. God loves them all, and each one of them is precious in his eyes. I admire Jackie's ministry and hope for the salvation of the people who fill the Walled City.

> Suppose someone has enough to live and sees a brother or sister in need, but does not help. Then God's love is not living in that person. (1 John 3:17)

Lord,

I've fallen behind in the stuff I need to get done. I pray that you would help me to be more disciplined this week and stay focused. Help me to manage my time more wisely. You can do anything; I believe that. So I ask that you would motivate me to keep moving forward in the things I need to do, and help me not to get overwhelmed.

> I can do all things through Christ, because he gives me strength. (Philippians 4:13)

JOURNAL OF
A SOUL SURFER

Through God, you *can* do anything; so what is it that you need to do? Make a list of the top priorities you'd like to focus on. Then make a list of any time wasters you need to avoid.

....

....

....

....

....

....

....

....

....

STDs

Casual sex has long-term effects. Not only do you lose your virginity, but you also set yourself up for health problems that can plague you the rest of your life. Lots of girls don't even know when they have a sexually transmitted disease such as HPV (human papillomavirus) or chlamydia. In fact, about 70 percent of women with chlamydia have no symptoms. But if left untreated, it can spread to all your reproductive organs and become pelvic inflammatory disease, which can lead to infertility. And HPV can lead to cervical cancer. Cancer! These are two gnarly diseases!

So before you decide to have sex with your boyfriend, think first about what the Bible says (save sex for marriage), and then think about whether you want to live with your decision the rest of your life.

A great resource for learning more about this is the book *What Every Parent Should Know About Teen Sex* by Becky Ettinger, RN, MSN. Nurse Becky is a great friend of my family and a solid Christian youth leader in California.

Make a Friend

When was the last time you made a new friend? Have you talked to someone you didn't know during a youth group activity? It's what Jesus would do. In fact, Jesus went out of his way to reach out to people who were rejected by others.

There is a story in the Bible about a man named Zacchaeus—a short, dishonest tax collector. He was hated by the people of his day because he cheated them. Jesus invited himself over to Zacchaeus's house to eat, and Zacchaeus became a changed man. He repaid everyone he had ever cheated.

It's easy to be nice to your friends. It's more challenging to step out of your comfort zone and make new friends. Do it for Jesus. Take the challenge!

> "And if you are nice only to your friends, you are no better than other people. Even those who don't know God are nice to their friends." (Matthew 5:47)

Serve One God

God tells us to serve him, not the gods of the people around us. That seems pretty easy seeing as we don't have too many stone or metal idols standing around (although there are a lot in our neighborhood). But other idols of today can be things such as popularity, fame, money, or people.

It's easy for me to idolize surfing. Often people put celebrities up on a pedestal, making fame their idol. Fortunately, I know and love the one true God. I don't want to hide the fact that he is the Lord of my life and the only One I worship.

Do you idolize things or people in your life? Or do you serve the one true God? You have the choice. "Choose for yourselves this day whom you will serve, whether the gods your forefathers served beyond the River, or the gods of the Amorites, in whose land you are living. But as for me and my household, we will serve the LORD" (Joshua 24:15). It's a daily decision.

> Fear the LORD Your God, serve him only . . . Do not
> follow other gods, the gods of the peoples around you.
> (Deuteronomy 6:13–14)

Partner Up!

Ever hear those words in school? Maybe in gym class or to work on a project in science or math class? God calls us to partner up as well. In Philippians, Paul thanks the Christians in Philippi for partnering with him to share the news of Jesus Christ.

I partner with World Vision and other organizations to help support children in countries where food and resources are scarce. You, too, can partner like this, but there are also many ways to partner with people or groups closer to home. Find a Christian organization you like, or even just help a local kid in your community.

You can get together with friends from church to pray for the missionaries your church supports or help out at a crisis pregnancy center. You can also partner with a teacher to help out in a class of younger kids. The possibilities are just about endless as you look for ways to serve God. Jesus said in Matthew 18:20, "This is true because if two or three people come together in my name, I am there with them." So partner up with someone else who is serving God, and do it together!

I thank God for the help you gave me while I preached the Good News—help you gave from the first day you believed until now. (Philippians 1:5)

EPIC RIDE

Working for God

Do you dream about doing something special for God? Would you like to try short- or long-term missionary work? Start your training at home, and see how you do:

1. Share Christ with your family and friends.
2. Volunteer in your community. Places to volunteer include soup kitchens, homeless shelters, crisis pregnancy centers, or programs where you can help teach kids to read.
3. Participate and/or attend the missions conference at your church. Host a missionary if your parents give the okay.
4. Practice being content where God has you now.
5. Read books about missionaries past and present.
6. Pray about where and how God would have you serve.
7. Participate in a short-term mission project through your church.

Jesus commissioned us: "You will be my witnesses—in Jerusalem [local], in all of Judea, in Samaria [national], and in every part of the world [international]" (Acts 1:8, words in brackets mine).

Just Thirteen!

Sometimes I wonder why God chose me.
After all, I was just a thirteen-year-old who loved to
surf. But age has nothing to do with it. God can call
anyone, and when he does, he gives that person the
strength she needs regardless of age or position.

Jeremiah had this same concern. When God called
him to share the word of the Lord with Israel, the first
thing Jeremiah said was, "I am only a child" (Jeremiah
1:6). God reassured Jeremiah that he was in charge and
would make him strong, protecting him even from the
armies of the king. Jeremiah ended up prophesying for
about forty years.

If God can use a teenager like Jeremiah, he can
certainly use me and you. All we need to do is be
open to the call and have faith that God is in control.
Challenging? Yes. But what a gift to be used by God.

> "Today I have made you a fortified city, an iron pillar and a
> bronze wall to stand against the whole land—against the
> kings of Judah, its officials, its priests and the people of
> the land. They will fight against you but will not overcome
> you, for I am with you and will rescue you," declares the
> LORD. (Jeremiah 1:18–19)

24/7 Open Line

Prayer is the ultimate open phone line.
God never sleeps, never goes off-line, and never has a
power outage. In fact, he's so eager to hear from you
that he rejoices in your voice. Prayer is the heart of
your relationship with God, so don't be a stranger.

I daily pray on my own but often with my parents
and friends as well. I talk to God about struggles I'm
facing and thank him for the good things (and bad) in
my life (Romans 8:28). I pray for my family, friends,
and other relationships. I pray about surfing contests,
traveling, and everything else you can think of!

I've learned many things about prayer. First, there
is no word or time limit for a prayer. Short prayers are
great, and long ones are great too. Second, prayer is
not hard. You don't have to use formal words. Prayer is
just a fancy word for talking to God. Just talk like you
normally do. Third, prayer is an important part of your
relationship with God. He commands you to pray and
wants you to as well. Fourth, a prayer journal helps.
You will really be motivated to pray when you see
answers to prayers. Write down your prayer requests—
even write down your prayers—and record how God
answers. Sometimes his answer is no. But keep your
heart and mind open to see what his greater plan is.
Whatever you do, pray all the time!

Pray continually. (1 Thessalonians 5:17)

Every Detail, Every Hair

God cares about your worries, fears, and needs. In fact, God cares so much that he tells you to give all your worries to him to carry for you. He does this because he loves you.

God knows what you need even before you ask. I've been watching a lot of cooking shows and am learning to make healthy, tasty food. My mom loves her cast-iron pans, but I've found them to be too heavy. I told her I'd like to buy some lighter pans to cook with. She chuckled and pulled out an almost brand-new, very expensive lightweight pan that a neighbor had given her the day before. We were amazed at how, even before I asked, God had provided what I needed.

Our lives are filled with millions of details. God works them all out for our benefit. He cares for every detail in your life.

> "But God even knows how many hairs you have on your head. Don't be afraid. You are worth much more than many sparrows." (Luke 12:7)

Winning for Jesus

I was really stoked to win my first national surfing championship—the 2005 NSSA Explorer Women's Title. I worked hard to prepare for the competition, and during the event I concentrated on doing my very best surfing.

Although winning is a great feeling, I know that it gives me only a brief happiness because worldly happiness isn't everlasting. The real reward for me will come when I hear my Father say the words, "You did well. You are a good and loyal servant. . . . Come and share my joy with me" (Matthew 25:21).

Yes, surfing prizes are great for a while, but my goal as a Christian is to honor Christ and have an eternal life with him. That's what I really look forward to.

> "Don't store treasures for yourselves here on earth where moths and rust will destroy them and thieves can break in and steal them. But store your treasures in heaven where they cannot be destroyed by moths or rest and where thieves cannot break in and steal them." (Matthew 6:19–20)

Aloha

Aloha is a Hawaiian word used for hello, good-bye, and love. But it means much more than that. The true Hawaiian meaning translates "God bless you." _Aloha_ meant so much to me after the shark attack. People from my church brought meals to my family; some even cleaned our house. People from all over the world sent letters and e-mails. And many of my friends visited me at the hospital. But what my family really appreciated more than anything else was prayer. We sure needed it. It was an incredible outpouring of _aloha_.

God is the definition of true _aloha_. He loves us with an incredible love that knows no boundaries. He sacrificed his Son, Jesus, knowing that some wouldn't accept or understand this gift. He extended _aloha_ anyway. What an awesome expression of love.

> But God shows his great love for us in this way: Christ died for us while we were still sinners. (Romans 5:8)

Trophies on the Shelves

I never surf to win prizes, but I've won prizes because I love to surf. The awards you get for competitions, whether big or small, all represent an accomplishment. But what they really stand for is consistent practice and intensive training.

God wants us to strive to have faith, a godly character, a forgiving heart, and ultimately a relationship with him. It's just as much work, probably even more, to achieve these things as it is to work on my surfing. But although achievements in surfing will last only a short time, faith and joy last for eternity.

> You know that in a race all the runners run, but only one gets the prize. So run to win! All those who compete in the games use self-control so they can win a crown. That crown is an earthly thing that lasts only a short time, but our crown will never be destroyed. (1 Corinthians 9:24–25)

Garbage In, Garbage Out

Ever heard of the concept "garbage in, garbage out"? Take, for example, your body. When you eat unhealthy food, which is pretty much garbage for your body (*garbage in*), you're eventually, if not right away, going to see bad health results (*garbage out*). But if you eat food that is really nutritious, you're going to have good health and see the benefits.

This concept is true not only for our physical health, but also for our minds and hearts as well. If we fill them with garbage, that's exactly what's going to come out in our thoughts, words, and actions. Unfortunately, there's a lot of garbage out there in our modern world—bad language on TV, immoral images all over the Internet, sex scenes in movies. Not to mention the things people say and do all around us. It takes a conscious effort to keep the trash from getting in. When it does, what comes out is not pretty.

The good news is that the reverse is true too. If we fill our minds with the good stuff (scriptures, positive music, uplifting stories—think Philippians 4:8), our words and thoughts will come out clean and uplifting too. "Truth in, truth out." "Love in, love out"—that's a concept I can live with.

Brothers and sisters, think about the things that are good and worthy of praise. Think about the things that are true and honorable and right and pure and beautiful and respected. (Philippians 4:8)

Blessed is the man who does not walk in the counsel of the wicked or stand in the way of sinners or sit in the seat of mockers. But his delight is in the law of the Lord, and on his law he meditates day and night. He is like a tree planted by streams of water, which yields its fruit in season and whose leaf does not wither. Whatever he does prospers. (Psalm 1:1–3)

Integrity

According to *Merriam-Webster's Collegiate Dictionary,* the word *integrity* is defined as a "firm adherence to a code of moral . . . values." To Christians, it means doing what is right, honest, and helpful before God. Here are some examples of integrity I've experienced in my own life:

- Returning a lost wallet with all the money left in it.
- Going back and paying for an item the store clerk forgot to charge me for.
- Keeping promises.
- Telling the truth, even when I don't feel like it.
- Making good choices with friends who aren't Christians.

God desires for his followers to live above reproach and not to sacrifice integrity for personal gain. In Matthew 25:40, Jesus said, "I tell you the truth, anything you did for even the least of my people here, you also did for me."

A Young Woman I Admire: Cassie Bernall

Cassie Bernall's life on earth ended with one word: "Yes." When Dylan Klebold and Eric Harris asked her if she believed in God, she knew the answer held her life in the balance. She didn't hesitate that day at Columbine High School.

Cassie hadn't always lived for God. She had been rebellious and strayed far from God. But her parents did everything they could to bring her back. Cassie did come back to God, and her life changed as she decided to live for him. Now, in her death, she has impacted many thousands of people. Her family started the Cassie Bernall Home for Children in Las Lajas, Honduras, in honor of Cassie, who wanted to deliver babies for a living. Now children with no families or homes are given love and safety.

I hope that each of you has an adult or friend willing to risk everything to keep you close to God, and I hope both you and I are willing to risk it all to live for God. A life lived for God is both an honor and a miracle.

> "I tell you the truth, you must accept the kingdom of God as if you were a little child, or you will never enter it." Then Jesus took the children in his arms, put his hands on them, and blessed them. (Mark 10:15–16)

PRAYER

Dear God,

I need to ask for forgiveness. I pray that you will forgive me for what I did wrong today. I ask, Lord, that you will help me learn from this and do what's right. I thank you that you are a loving and forgiving God. And I pray that you would remind me to offer that same forgiveness to others.

With you there is forgiveness. (Psalm 130:4)

JOURNAL OF A SOUL SURFER

Forgiveness is a blessing from God. Recognize what you need to ask forgiveness for. First ask God; then think about who else needs to hear you say "I'm sorry; please forgive me." God also wants us to forgive others, just as He has done for us. Who needs to hear you say "I forgive you"?

....

....

....

....

....

....

....

....

Spread the Word

One of my favorite role models is Father Damien. He was a priest in the mid-1800s who came to the Hawaiian island of Molokai to work in a leper colony at Kalaupapa. He loved and ministered to those outcasts destined for a horrible death. Father Damien eventually died of leprosy as well. His life was dedicated to spreading the news of Jesus Christ through one-on-one contact with hurting people.

That's what Jesus taught us to do. Someone contacted my family about a boy named Logan who had lost his arm in an accident. I talked to him one day to find out how he was doing and to encourage him not to give up his dreams. You see, Logan is a really good competitive wakeboarder, and after we spoke that day, he got back out there on his wakeboard and kept ripping! God wants all of us to make the effort to reach out to people with his love, which is not always easy to do. It's hard to know what to say to people sometimes. Just be yourself, and God will give you the words to say.

Our faith isn't about keeping it to ourselves. It's about sharing what Jesus has done for us with the people around us every day. It's about talking, hugging, calling, sharing, and caring.

My brothers and sisters, if people say they have faith, but do nothing, their faith is worth nothing. Can faith like that save them? (James 2:14)

The Blessing and a Curse

Being sort of well-known has its blessings.
I like being able to encourage other people. I like being able to help people who need it, such as supporting organizations that dig wells for communities in Africa so the people can have clean water. I also like being able to talk about Christ. But being well-known can also have its downside. Sometimes when I just want to keep to myself, people will recognize me and want to say hi.

Whether people recognize me or not doesn't change who I am in God's eyes, and it doesn't change what he expects from me. The bottom line is that I'm just like everyone else in God's eyes. He loves me enough to die for me, he wants me to obey him because of my love for him, and he wants me to love others as he has loved me.

He hopes the same for you. It doesn't matter whether you're famous or the quietest kid on the planet. God's love and respect is equal for each person. His love is unconditional. And he hopes you will reflect his love toward others.

> "The greatest love a person can show is to die for his friends." (John 15:13)

EPIC RIDE

Ten Ways to Celebrate Jesus

1. Die to self. Do something unselfishly for someone else.
2. Live for Jesus. In everything you do, do it for his glory. He can use you!
3. Hunt down positive, uplifting movies, and watch them with friends (The Chronicles of Narnia, *Amistad, The Mission, Lady Jane, Pollyanna, A Walk to Remember, End of the Spear, The Blind Side, Soul Surfer*).
4. Take a walk by yourself. Really enjoy God's creation and pray.
5. Treat your friend to a makeover: polish her nails, style her hair, give her a facial and a foot and neck massage.
6. Simplify your life, and detoxify your room of clutter.
7. Pretend you're cooking for Jesus, and make a three-course dinner for your youth leader.
8. Begin journaling your thoughts, struggles, and prayers. Buy a beautiful journal to start with.
9. Go out of your way to help someone else. It could be your mom, a neighbor, or someone you don't know.
10. Meditate on God's love for you, and thank him for the many gifts he's given you. Memorize John 16:27: "The Father himself loves you." Share it with a friend.

Goodwill Ambassador

Rip Curl is my surfing sponsor. That means I promote their company by wearing Rip Curl clothing, appearing in their ads, and surfing my best. It's a win-win situation for all of us because they provide me with clothing and other surfing necessities, and I help advertise for them. They sponsored me before the attack, but I didn't know if they would sponsor me afterward. They were very supportive, though, and wanted to keep me on their team. I'm a little like an ambassador for the surfing culture and the Rip Curl brand.

I'm more than a surfing ambassador though. I'm an ambassador for Christ. Just as people recognize me as a surfer, I hope I represent Jesus even more than surfing. An ambassador's role is to represent someone else, and my role as a believer in Jesus is to represent him.

Being ambassadors for Christ isn't easy. Sometimes we are the only representative of Christ that a person sees. If we mess up by being selfish or mean or using bad language, Christ's reputation is tainted. I take my role as ambassador for Christ seriously. I hope you do too.

So we have been sent to speak for Christ. It is as if God is calling to you through us. We speak for Christ when we beg you to be at peace with God. (2 Corinthians 5:20)

God Sees the Bad Stuff

There's so much bad stuff in the world as a result of sin. There is war, where innocent people become victims. There are diseases such as AIDS and cancer, which affect millions of people every year. There are numerous accounts of starvation, poverty, abuse, persecution, and death here in the United States and around the world.

When you think about all the bad stuff, it's hard to remember that God is actively working for good in this world. God sees those who are hungry and hurting and abused, and he loves them. He also sends people like you and me to help demonstrate his love to them.

The bad stuff happens because of sin. When sin came into this world, so did heartache and trouble. But God hates sin. He sent Jesus to defeat it and asks us to overcome it through him. What a great reason to be a part of the good things God is doing through his people. God calls us to be his hands and feet; it's our job to make a difference as he leads.

Here are some obvious ways to make a difference, but ask God how he wants you to help personally:

1. Support a missionary.
2. Feed and care for orphans.

3. Raise funds for the starving in Africa (or somewhere else).

But you, O God, do see trouble and grief; you consider it to take it in hand. The victim commits himself to you; you are the helper of the fatherless. (Psalm 10:14)

Light vs. Darkness

Sun is a major part of my life. I wear sunscreen all the time, and T-shirts while surfing, to protect my skin from ultraviolet rays. Sometimes I avoid surfing in the middle of the day because the sun glaring off the water can be dangerous for my eyes. But as bright as the Hawaiian sun is, the light of God is so much brighter. God brings light to dark places, but it's more than just brightening a room or a face. God's light reveals what was hidden in the darkness of our hearts. And he destroys it when we accept him as Savior. As Christians, God's light should shine through us every day.

When I was little, I loved to sing "This Little Light of Mine." One of the verses says, "Hide it under a bushel. No!" God wants us to shine with such spiritual brightness that we illuminate others around us. Matthew 5:14–16 says that we are the light of the world—like a city on a mountain, glowing in the night for all to see. So instead of hiding your light under a basket, put it on a stand. Let your good deeds shine for all to see. Don't hide God's light.

How can you shine brightly for God?

- Have a good attitude even when circumstances are difficult—focus on the long-term.

- Love others with his unconditional love. Treat them as you would like to be treated.
- Proudly proclaim your love for Jesus.
- Obey God.

"So be careful not to let the light in you become darkness. If your whole body is full of light, and none of it is dark, then you will shine bright, as when a lamp shines on you." (Luke 11:35–36)

The Secret to Winning

Sometimes I wonder what the secret is to winning a surfing competition. For me, a combination of having consistent training, a highly developed skill level, motivation, a good attitude, and a plan has usually worked to get me to the top of my game. But, especially with surfing, other elements come into play that you personally can't control.

I think those same ideas apply to the Christian life. *Victory* means developing your walk with Christ (skills), loving God with all your heart (attitude), and letting God control your life (plan). It's tempting to work really hard on mastering skills (just ask the religious leaders of Jesus' day), but it's more difficult to have a right attitude and rely on and trust in God's plan for your life. The ultimate goal is to be the best we can be personally and let God direct our lives.

Set some goals for yourself. First, work on your attitude. Are you really seeking to please God? Or do you want to control everything? Along with attitude, work on other skills such as patience, perseverance, faith, and joy. You're putting together a winning combination in his eyes.

In all the work you are doing, work the best you can.
Work as if you were doing it for the Lord, not for people.
(Colossians 3:23)

Cheating

Cheating is a form of lying. It breaks the ninth commandment (Exodus 20:16). People from all walks of life are guilty of cheating. Kids cheat on tests and homework at school all the time, and people cheat on each other. A 2004 study called "Report Card on the Ethics of American Youth" (www.familyeducation.com) found that 74 percent of students admitted cheating on a test at least once within the past year, 93 percent had lied to their parents, and 83 percent had lied to their teachers.

Are you a cheater? It seems so easy to cheat, but the person who gets hurt most is you. When you cheat, you don't learn what you need to in school, and you don't have the satisfaction of achievement or having decent relationships. And worst of all, you hurt God.

Just repent! Turn from your sin, and choose this day whom you will honor and obey.

What Does the Future Hold?

I don't know what the future is going to be like, but I know the safe place to be is close to Jesus. I could get married and have five kids and teach them all to surf. I could go to Bible college in a couple of years and end up leading an organization that helps underprivileged kids. I could live at home, taking care of my parents and making surfing videos. Who knows? Only God.

The good thing is that I don't have to know everything right now. His everyday plan for me is to be his hands and feet wherever I go. He guides me one step at a time, one day at a time. My passion is to seek him every day, be open to what he wants me to do, and express his love to whomever he puts in my path.

It's very reassuring to know that God has a plan for my future. He also has one for your future. Let him be your loving Father, and see where he guides you!

"Seek first God's kingdom and what God wants. Then all your other needs will be met as well. So don't worry about tomorrow, because tomorrow will have its own worries. Each day has enough trouble of its own." (Matthew 6:33–34)

Second Chances

Jonah is a great example of God's second chances. He was a prophet when God told him to go to Nineveh and preach to that sinful city. Instead, Jonah fled the other way. When a storm threatened the ship he was on, Jonah realized it was God trying to get his attention. He told the sailors to throw him overboard. When they did, the storm stopped, but Jonah was swallowed by a huge fish. After three days the fish coughed Jonah up onto the land, and he repented and decided he'd better obey God.

Jonah obeyed God by preaching to the people about repentance and God's wrath. The whole city repented, and God forgave and spared them. This story displays God's love and forgiveness for everyone. First, God allowed Jonah to repent. Then he allowed Nineveh to repent, and the entire city followed the Lord—one of history's greatest revivals.

God only wants the best for us and will do what it takes to inspire and correct us. His love never fails.

> I knew that you are a gracious and compassionate God, slow to anger and abounding in love, a God who relents from sending calamity. (Jonah 4:2)

Women I Admire: Esther

Esther started out a young Jewish orphan and ended up a chosen queen. God placed her in that position so he could use her to save the Jewish people from annihilation. Here's Esther's story in quick form: King Xerxes needed a new queen, so a beauty pageant was held for him to choose one. Among the most beautiful girls in the land, he chose Esther. Haman, Xerxes' right-hand man, hated Jews, especially Mordecai, Esther's cousin. Haman devised a plan to kill all the Jews; Mordecai told Esther; and Esther told the king. Haman was killed, and the Jews were saved.

Esther was an amazing woman because she risked her life to stop Haman's evil plan. She heard there was something going on that was against God, and she took action to stop it. Of course she was scared, because the king could have had her killed when she walked into his presence without his permission. But the love God had given her for her people gave her the courage to stand up for what was right. She used her position as queen to accomplish something amazing for God.

God's purpose is to use each one of us in both big and small ways. Every act of love honors him— whether it's for an entire nation or for your pesky little brother.

For if you remain silent at this time, relief and deliverance for the Jews will arise from another place, but you and your father's family will perish. And who knows but that you have come to royal position for such a time as this? (Esther 4:14)

Why Not Me?

The thought has crossed my mind, *Why me?* Why did that shark have to attack me? I'm just a girl who loves to surf. What do I have to offer the world? But knowing God, a better question is, *Why not me?*

God calls all of us to do amazing things for him. He called fishermen to be Jesus' disciples, he called tax collectors and carpenters and prostitutes, and he used shepherds and children to proclaim his message. Why wouldn't he use a surfer girl? Why wouldn't he use you?

God asks us to go outside our comfort zones to do things for him, to reach out in love and help others. Whether you're a missionary in a country far from home or have a job at a local restaurant, God calls you to live out your salvation regardless of the circumstances. God also promises to give us the strength to do what he asks. So be ready to do whatever God asks. I can promise you it will be amazing.

> My sons, do not be negligent now, for the LORD has chosen you to stand before him and serve him, to minister before him. (2 Chronicles 29:11)

Lord,

I thank you for my future husband and pray that he will stay pure and strong in you and that he would grow to have a genuine love for you. Guard his heart and mind every day. Help him to turn to you when he's struggling. And bless him today, wherever and whoever he may be.

> Do not worry about anything, but pray and ask God for everything you need, always giving thanks. (Philippians 4:6)

JOURNAL OF A SOUL SURFER

Maybe someone is praying for you, or the *future* you, right now! How can you guard your own heart to keep it pure? Ask God to help you stay pure and strong now for the future he has waiting for you.

....

....

....

....

....

....

....

....

EPIC RIDE

Random Acts of Kindness

1. Write an encouraging note to a teacher, a youth leader, or your pastor.
2. Write a letter or send an e-mail to your grandparents who live far away.
3. Secretly take out the trash without being asked.
4. Offer to scrape the snow and ice off cars in the church parking lot.
5. Share your umbrella with someone who doesn't have one.
6. Offer to rake leaves or shovel snow for your neighbor who works all day.
7. Bring flowers to your friend who is going through a hard time.
8. Give up soda for one month, and send the fifteen dollars to orphans in Sudan.
9. Help your younger siblings with their homework—without complaining!
10. Take the cart back for a shopper in the grocery store parking lot.

In all the work you are doing, work the best you can.
Work as if you were doing it for the Lord, not for people.
(Colossians 3:23)

The Body Is Weak

The first time I got back on my surfboard
after the attack, I had some physical struggles to face.
I hadn't surfed in almost four weeks, so I was a little
out of shape. Plus, I had never been forced to function
in the water with only one arm. I had every intention
of surfing at the top of my game, but my body didn't
know what to do right away to compensate for the loss
of an arm—except to fall a lot more than usual.

One day when I was back on my surfboard, I chose
to work hard on my weaknesses so that I could figure
out how to make my body do what it needed to do to
catch and ride waves. I trained my body in a new way
to accommodate having only one arm, and I worked
hard to get my balance back. But it took time and many
wipeouts.

I think we all face similar struggles in our spiritual
lives. When we are spiritually out of shape, our
spiritual body is weak and out of practice—which
makes it easier to fall into temptation and struggle
with a bad attitude and an unloving heart. Just as
it is important to be physically fit and healthy, it
is important to regain your spiritual health today
and train to stay in shape. Spiritual training means
spending time in prayer and Bible study so that you
can learn to react like Jesus would. If you train yourself
to react like Jesus would, it will become more natural

in your everyday character. And you will honor God by doing this.

> "Stay awake and pray for strength against temptation. The spirit wants to do what is right, but the body is weak." (Mark 14:38)

Used, Not Abused

My mom and I were praying in the days and weeks before the shark attack that God would use me to do something great for him. Of course I never thought it would be like this. Although the attack was terrifying and the future seemed uncertain, I had this underlying knowledge that God was going to use it for his glory.

It seems weird, but I'm honored that God trusted me enough to use me. Paul thanked God for considering him faithful enough to use him to spread the news of Jesus. I'm thankful that God considered me faithful enough to appoint me to his service.

No matter who you are, God can use you. You might think otherwise, and I did too, but then the attack happened. I thought to myself, *Here I am just thirteen, and there God goes using me.*

> I thank Christ Jesus our Lord, who gave me strength, because he trusted me and gave me this work of serving him. (1 Timothy 1:12)

Motivated by Love

My family doesn't hide our faith in God.
We talk about God all the time with each other and
with friends. As surfers, we have met other Christian
surfers around the world and enjoy fellowshipping
with them wherever we go. We're not afraid to pray in
public. We listen to Christian music, and our house is
full of CDs by Christian bands such as P.O.D., Hillsong,
and Bethany Dillon. We love to read the Bible and enjoy
watching good, clean movies.

We do these things because we are excited about
Jesus and can't get enough of God's love. We want
to see him work, learn more about him, and fill our
minds with thoughts that glorify him.

I heard this story about some people in South
Africa at a Christian outreach who, during the altar
call, ran down to the altar to surrender their lives to
Jesus and become saved. They saw a glimpse of God's
love and recognized the truth in the message. They
could not wait to be a part of the exciting journey that
lay before them.

That's how my family and I feel about Jesus. It's
so exciting to be a part of what God is doing in this
world in people's lives. So don't be ashamed of your
love for him.

"You are the light that gives light to the world. A city that is built on a hill cannot be hidden. . . . In the same way, you should be a light for other people. Live so that they will see the good things you do and will praise your Father in heaven." (Matthew 5:14, 16)

WIPEOUT

Promises, Promises

God has never broken a promise. Keeping a promise is a serious thing. Say you promise your little sister you'll do her hair in French braids, and then you don't have time to do it. She's crushed, and you have broken your promise. Say you promise your parents you'll be home by 11:00 p.m., but you show up at 1:30 a.m. You've broken your promise to them, and they've lost trust in you.

God made lots of promises to his people. He promised Noah he would never again flood the entire earth. He promised Abraham that he would be the father of a huge nation. God promised Israel that if they followed his rule, he would protect them. And he is fulfilling those promises even to this day.

God never goes back on his promises. Why? Because God is God. Nehemiah, the great rebuilder of Jerusalem, said, "You have kept your promise because you are righteous" (Nehemiah 9:8).

As Christians, we need to keep the promises we make so we don't appear hypocritical and so others will trust the One we follow. If there's a promise you can't keep, don't make it!

Faith Meets Real Life

Hawaii is known for its trade winds. And just like I have never seen those winds, I have never seen God. But the reality that winds exist is pretty obvious because of the evidence—tree branches sway, hair blows, my wet skin cools. The reality of God is also obvious. Although God is not someone you can see physically, like you see your family or friends, you can see God through his creation and the evidence of his power in people's lives. That's where faith comes in. The Bible says faith is knowing that something is real even if we do not see it.

A friend who visited my message board linked faith to God's never leaving us. She quoted Psalm 9:10, which says that God has "never forsaken those who seek" him. That's a pretty powerful combination. I have faith in God's existence even though I can't see him, and the Bible confirms that God is real and will never leave me. So I know God is right beside me as I live each day.

This knowledge changes the way I live. He knows not only what I do but also what my intentions are in doing it. That could be scary. But I know God is there for a reason. He'll give me strength when I need it and correct me when I have done wrong. He's for real, and I can't deny it.

> Faith means being sure of the things we hope for and knowing that something is real even if we do not see it. (Hebrews 11:1)

A Willing Heart

Mary was a humble Jewish girl. She
probably did as she was told, respected her parents,
and blended into the crowd in the small town of
Nazareth. But God, in his wisdom, made her his choice
for this unique, divine task. She had a yielded spirit and
a willing heart. She is described in Scripture as having
a heart of worship and a strong, faithful trust in God.
No wonder God chose her. Mary was willing to do what
seemed miraculous: give birth to the Son of God.

I'd like to have the same kind of willing heart Mary
had. She was willing to risk her fiancé's rejection,
encounter the scorn of the townspeople, and face her
parents' possible disappointment to follow God. I want
to be willing to risk everything to follow God. I want to
say yes to being used by him.

Think about your own life. What will you risk to
follow God? Are you willing to give up the things that
hold you back from serving him more? Do you yield to
God's plan and direction?

Mary said, "I am the servant of the Lord. Let this happen to
me as you say!" Then the angel went away. (Luke 1:38)

Every Day for God

Living for Jesus is not a once-a-week thing. It's not even a when-I'm-in-trouble thing. Living for Jesus is a 24/7 thing. One of the reasons you need to live for Jesus every minute is because Satan is trying every minute to defeat you. He never rests in his quest to fill the world (and you) with evil.

To overcome evil, you need to be on God's side all the time. This means putting Jesus first in your life, avoiding tempting situations and people, and filling your time "doing good" (as it says in Romans 12:21).

Here are some examples of "doing good": helping those in need, living peacefully with others, being happy despite troubles, being thankful for God's gifts to you. This is not a list of things you must do to make God happy; it's a list of how you can live with God's joy in your life. Living for Jesus isn't just about following a bunch of random commandments. It's an attitude of the heart that defeats evil every time.

> Do not let evil defeat you, but defeat evil by doing good.
> (Romans 12:21)

True Courage

Mildred "Babe" Didrikson Zaharias
earned gold medals in track and field in the 1932
Olympics, then went on to become a professional
golfer. She won eighty-two tournaments in her
career, including five (one the U.S. Open) after she
was diagnosed with cancer. She died in 1956 at age
forty-five.

The United States Sports Academy awards its
Mildred "Babe" Didrikson Zaharias Courage Award
every year, and they presented me with that award in
2005. Being recognized here and all over the world for
coming back to surfing after the attack is a big honor
for me that is best left at the foot of the cross. The
courage it took to return to competitive surfing after
the attack is nothing compared to the courage it takes
to be a follower of God and to share the gospel.

Paul and Timothy had plenty of opportunities to
be afraid as they traveled to spread the good news
of Jesus. It was dangerous: people were stoned and
tortured and arrested for preaching about Jesus. In
fact, Paul wrote his letter to the Philippian Christians
while he was in jail. Instead of complaining, Paul
prayed that he would have the courage to keep telling
people about God no matter what circumstances came
his way.

Jesus also is a great example of courage. He quietly

submitted as he was led to his death as payment for our sins—himself innocent of all crimes. He had the courage to pay the ultimate price.

Take courage in the little challenges in your life. When the big ones come your way, it will be easier to respond courageously.

> Be strong and courageous, and do the work. Do not be afraid or discouraged, for the LORD God, my God, is with you. He will not fail you or forsake you. (1 Chronicles 28:20)

EPIC RIDE

Helping Other Believers

Galatians 6:10 says we should help others, especially those who are fellow believers. Here are a few ways to help out at your church:

1. Volunteer to do an art project with a Sunday school class.
2. Plant potted flowers, and sell them at your next church fund-raiser instead of unhealthy snacks and sweets.
3. Spend some time cleaning up the youth room with your friends after church.
4. Pray for your youth group, youth leaders, and friends. See how God answers those prayers.
5. Be the first to welcome a new person in your youth group, and then get to know her.
6. Team up with some friends to teach a children's Sunday school class.
7. Greet the new kids you see entering your church building, and invite them to the Sunday school classes or youth group.
8. Grab some friends, and clean the house of an elderly person or someone who is ill.
9. Prepare a great meal with your friends for a new mom or for someone who is ill.
10. Get artistic with your friends and decorate some of the Sunday school classrooms.

Can I Stir That for You?

I recently sat on a plane mixing a powdered nutrition drink. As I clumsily stirred, I managed to get the mixture all over myself, the tray, and the arm rest.

Meanwhile, an older man was sitting behind me observing. Finally he couldn't take it anymore and offered to stir it for me. I immediately said "no thanks" because I just prefer to do things on my own and I was almost done. He said it was agony watching me stir. Ha ha! I laughed and said "don't watch!" and finished stirring. I again smiled and said "don't watch!" I hope he didn't watch because I did an awful job stirring. I finished my drink happily and went on with my flight.

Later I began thinking that as we face difficulties in our lives, God is probably watching with regret, wishing we would allow him to help us "stir our drinks." He can definitely do a much better job with our challenges than we can, but first we need to hand them over to him.

Cast your cares on the LORD and he will sustain you; he will never let the righteous fall. (Psalm 55:22)

What's Slowing You Down?

Part of being a good surfer is having confidence in your equipment and your own skills and strengths. Not enough wax on your board, having the wrong type of surfboard for the conditions, or a leash that is about to break will destroy your confidence and keep you from performing at your peak.

It's the same with our spiritual lives. Lack of prayer can slow down our walk with God; so can not spending time reading the Bible. Putting surfing or friends before God can mean a spiritual wipeout later. But the real deadweight that disables us is sin. I don't like it when my spiritual walk is more like a slow crawl.

All of us need to make sure that anything slowing down our spiritual lives is kicked out of the way. Prayer, Bible reading, and encouragement from others can help us figure out what is slowing us down. God will help us remove it from our path.

> We are surrounded by a great cloud of people whose lives tell us what faith means. So let us run the race that is before us and never give up. We should remove from our lives anything that would get in the way and the sin that so easily holds us back. (Hebrews 12:1)

The Power of Prayer

Right after getting bitten by the shark,
the first thing I did was pray. I prayed that God would
keep me alive, that he would help me get to shore, and
that he would help me through the ordeal. And he did!

One of the most amazing things he did was keep
me calm. Most people probably would have freaked out
and panicked after having an arm bitten off by a shark.
But God answered my prayers and kept me calm and
gave me his peace. He truly guarded my heart against
panic.

The doctors later told me that staying calm
contributed to my survival. Because I didn't panic and
start screaming and thrashing around, my heart didn't
beat faster, which means I didn't lose as much blood.
I'm alive today thanks to God's care. When in the midst
of a crisis, peace comes from knowing you can call on
such a powerful God.

> Do not worry about anything, but pray and ask God for
> everything you need, always giving thanks. And God's
> peace, which is so great we cannot understand it, will keep
> your hearts and minds in Christ Jesus. (Philippians 4:6–7)

Who's Your Savior?

The days and weeks following the shark attack weren't always easy for me or my family. I was physically weakened by the loss of blood and worried about the future (at least my parents were). I was a little scared too. I had so much support from my friends and family, but I also knew God was by my side every moment with every detail before, during, and after the attack. And I know he'll be there in all of my tomorrows.

Jesus Christ saved me from eternity in hell when he died on the cross. But he also saved me on October 31, 2003, when I almost died from the shark attack. God's strength and encouragement—which saved me from discouragement—was revealed through the support and prayers of my family, friends, and many other people I didn't even know. Throughout the rest of my life, he will continue to save me from making bad choices and throwing my life away.

The apostle Paul experienced some pretty rough times. In the book of 2 Corinthians, Paul said that God had saved him from death and that God would continue to save him. Paul depended on God's strength, and it was enough.

Can you save yourself? No. Wisdom means knowing your limits and knowing when to call on your Savior for help in times of need.

Truly, in our own hearts we believed we would die. But this happened so we would not trust in ourselves but in God, who raises people from the dead. God saved us from these great dangers of death, and he will continue to save us. We have put our hope in him, and he will save us again. (2 Corinthians 1:9–10)

The Greatest Dad Ever

I love my dad. He's been an awesome influence on me since I was a little girl. He took me to church, where I learned about God, but he also influenced me through his own testimony and life for Christ. He's a great and loving dad who's very supportive of me and my surfing!

As much as I love my dad, I love my heavenly Father too. As much as I love being my dad's only daughter, I love being God's child too. Remember when you were little and your dad would snuggle you on his lap and read books to you or just sit with you? God treats us the same way. He protects us and cares for us, wrapping his arms around us in love.

I know some of you don't have a dad in your life. Maybe you never knew your dad, or maybe your parents are divorced so you don't see your dad much, or maybe your dad has died. God can fill that role as your heavenly Father. He waits here, asking to fill your life with the blessings of his love. He wants to give you the desires of your heart when you choose to trust and follow him. You are his child, and he loves you. Let him wrap his arms around you and bring you close to his heart.

I will be your father, and you will be my sons and daughters, says the Lord Almighty. (2 Corinthians 6:18)

EPIC RIDE

Ten Inspiring Biographies

1. *Through Gates of Splendor* by Elisabeth Elliot
2. *The Heavenly Man* by Brother Yun with Paul Hattaway
3. *Bruchko* by Bruce Olson and James L. Lund
4. *Gladys Aylward: The Adventure of a Lifetime* by Janet and Geoff Benge
5. *She Said Yes: The Unlikely Martyrdom of Cassie Bernall* by Misty Bernall
6. *The Hiding Place* by Corrie ten Boom
7. *Chasing the Dragon* by Jackie Pullinger
8. *God's Smuggler* by Brother Andrew
9. *The Cross and the Switchblade* by David Wilkerson
10. *Run, Baby, Run* by Nicky Cruz

Skittles

Have you ever done something wrong
and felt guilty about it? I have. When I was in the sixth
grade, my friends and I stole some Skittles candy out
of a big jar in the cafeteria at school. The Skittles were
there to reward certain kids for doing special things.
We ended up getting caught and had to clean all the
cafeteria tables for one week. I felt so guilty for what I
had done. I still have feelings of guilt over stealing the
candy to this day. I never want to steal anything else
ever again.

When you're a Christian, the Holy Spirit lives in
you. He is there to teach you and remind you of the
things God has taught. In John 14:26, Jesus said, "But
the Helper will teach you everything and will cause
you to remember all that I told you. This Helper is the
Holy Spirit whom the Father will send in my name."

So my remembrance of this event and the guilt I
felt is the Holy Spirit reminding me that it is wrong to
steal. I thank God for the presence of his Holy Spirit in
my life. It has kept me out of trouble. And I know that
God forgives me.

You shall not steal. (Exodus 20:15)

Ticked Off

Before many of the interviews and shows I have done, people have tried to tell me to keep God out of the conversation. But how can I? He is involved in every aspect of my life. Maybe they think God isn't real or shouldn't be mentioned in public. Or maybe they think a teenager doesn't have enough knowledge to talk about God.

Our calling as Christians is to bring more people to the kingdom of God by sharing his love and what he has to offer. We need to take that opportunity any time we can.

Don't get ticked off and frustrated if someone tries to stop you from sharing. Ask God to give you wisdom, the right words to share, and compassion for those skeptical about God.

> I am not ashamed of the Good News, because it is the power God uses to save everyone who believes. (Romans 1:16)

The Usual Questions (just so you know)

Q: Did it hurt when the shark bit you?

A: No. When I was on *Oprah*, one of the other guests was a doctor. He shared that the mind can shut down the pain sensor in your brain if it's necessary for your survival.

Q: Did you see the shark?

A: I didn't see it come or go. I felt a tug, turned my head, and saw a gray blur slip back into the ocean. It was that quick.

Q: Aren't you afraid of the water?

A: I've been playing in the water since I was four; why would I be afraid of the water? Of course I'm cautious of the dangers in the ocean, and I do my best to make smart decisions. My passion and love for surfing far outweigh my fear.

Q: What TV shows have you been on?

A: Honestly this stuff doesn't really matter to me. But if you need to know . . . *20/20*, *Good Morning America*, *The Today Show*, CNN, Outdoor Life Network, *Entertainment Tonight*, *The 700 Club* on TBN, *Oprah*, *Extreme Makeover: Home Edition*, ESPN, *Inside Edition*, and *TRL* on MTV. I have a cool story about that one. On *TRL*, when the host asked me my motivation for my comeback, I responded, "Jesus!" The audience stood up and cheered. It was such an awesome moment!

Oh, Brother!

When people ask me why I'm so competitive, I blame it on my two older brothers. After all, I wanted to keep up with everything they did. But it's more than just competition between us. I really admire these guys!

Noah, the oldest, is a great stand-up surfer and an amazing photographer. He's taken most of the pictures we have of me surfing. He's also very focused and determined in everything he does. My brother Tim is between Noah and me. He's a bodyboarder and videographer. He also makes us laugh a lot with his subtle sense of humor. Both of my brothers help me with their computer and photography skills, and they look out for me just as much as they tease me and pick on me.

Growing up, Noah and Tim avidly attended almost all of the Christian youth group events on the island, sought out and found solid Christian music, and tried to make good choices in their everyday lives. My brothers are great examples to me just by living their lives for God and not the world.

And God gave us this command: Those who love God must also love their brothers and sisters. (1 John 4:21)

Strict Training

In training and in life, I've found you only get out of it what you put into it. Many elements play a part in building a strong athlete, and it's the same when developing the heart of a Christian:

Strong Athlete	Christian Heart
Healthy, well-balanced nutrition	Reading the Word
Physical training	Teaching and serving others
Coach's advice	Spiritual mentor's guidance
Team support and pushing each other	Christian fellowship, accountability, and inspiring each other
Mental training	Prayer and trust in God

We can't expect physical results or spiritual results if we don't dedicate ourselves to the right training. It's always worth it in the end.

Everyone who competes in the games goes into strict training. They do it to get a crown that will not last; but we do it to get a crown that will last forever. (1 Corinthians 9:25 NIV)

Don't Stop Trying

The first time I got back on the surfboard after the attack was challenging. I didn't have two arms to paddle into the waves like I was used to, and standing up on the board with one arm was not easy at first either. I wiped out a few times before I finally got the right combination of momentum, hand placement, and balance. I kept trying until I caught a wave, stood up, and rode.

The biggest thing I needed to do was not give up. If I'd given up after the first two attempts, I wouldn't be surfing like I am today. Not giving up is important in a lot of areas of life. Playing an instrument takes practice; learning a language does too. Taking a chemistry class, learning to do a flip on a trampoline, or even getting along with your siblings can take practice.

Growing in your faith takes practice too. If living for God were easy, we'd all be doing it. Instead, God asks us to do difficult things such as have patience, love our enemies, and trust God completely. God tells us never to stop trying. So don't. Get on that board one more time!

> Think about Jesus' example. He held on while wicked people were doing evil things to him. So do not get tired and stop trying. (Hebrews 12:3)

Motivation

Someone once asked me what my motivation is for what I do. After thinking about this question, I realized what motivates everyone to do what they do—love. For me, I love surfing, and I love Jesus. My love for both motivates many of my actions. Because I love surfing and strive to excel at it, I am motivated to do things that will help me accomplish that goal: surf for practice and training; eat healthy; exercise to stay in shape; study waves, conditions, and water safety; and compete in surfing competitions.

In the same way—because I love Jesus and have experienced God's love for me—I want to live for him and am motivated to form my actions around that goal. In order for me to live for Jesus, though, I need to know how he would want me to live. So I study the Bible and seek God for guidance and direction. Along the way, he teaches me.

Part of my motivation for living for Jesus is seeing him work in my life and in other people's lives. Seeing what God is doing and being in total agreement with his plan makes me passionate to be a part of whatever he will do next. It makes me to want to please him in everything I do.

God gave me that love for surfing so I could use it for his glory. Thank God for giving us love and passion

for the things we each enjoy. Use the love and passion he has given you for that special thing to further his kingdom.

> The Father has loved us so much that we are called children of God. And we really are his children. The reason the people in the world do not know us is that they have not known him. (1 John 3:1)

Heaven on Earth

One day heaven will descend to earth, and God's children will live forever in the most glorious city ever. The river of the Water of Life will flow down the middle of the city, and there will be no sun or moon or night because God is the light. God and his Son, Jesus, will live there, along with the angels and those who followed Christ in this life.

Can you imagine such a beautiful place? It will be made of gold and precious stones and jewels, with gates of pearl. Despite all this, its beauty will be secondary. What is most important is the fact that we will be in the presence of Almighty God. There will be no death, disease, depression; no pain, loss, anger, or regret. Those living in heaven will never experience the bad things that fill our world. We will be there to worship our King!

I don't know if I'll live in heaven with both of my arms or not, but I don't think it will matter. I'll just be happy to be surrounded by God's presence and love in his holy city. I like where I live now. Kauai is beautiful, but it's nothing like heaven will be. I look forward to living with God, and I know I will because I've accepted him as my Savior and I live each day for him. I pray that one day you will experience the love and salvation of the one true God. If you would like to, the Bible says in Acts 2:21, "Then anyone who calls on

the Lord will be saved." So I can't wait to meet you in heaven, and we will be friends forever!

> He will wipe away every tear from their eyes, and there will be no more death, sadness, crying, or pain, because all the old ways are gone. (Revelation 21:4)

EPIC RIDE

Five Good Habits to Build into Your Daily Life

1. *Bible study and prayer.* Start out simple. Read from Psalms or Proverbs every day, and share your heart with your best friend—God.

2. *Exercise.* Get yourself moving every day. Find your passion. Try walking, in-line skating, or running.

3. *Healthy eating.* Eat foods that are as natural as possible—the way God made them.

4. *Kindness.* Be nice to your friends and family, but remember that random acts of kindness are great too. Let God's love and kindness shine through you.

5. *Quietness.* You don't need to be busy every second or have your music cranked all the time. Sit quietly, and listen to God speak. I like sitting quietly on the beach, listening to the crashing waves and the wind blowing through the trees.

Staying Focused

My life has become very public since the attack, and I could never do what I now do without having a strong relationship with my loving heavenly Father. I always call upon him for everything, and he has shown me that if I just stay by his side, I can do all things through Christ who strengthens me.

With all the stuff going on in my life (surfing, training, competition, interviews, appearances), it gets really busy, and sometimes I let busyness rule my life and become more important than other things (like spending time with God). For example, as I grow older and get busier, I have found that reading the Bible every day has *not* been easy. There have been times when I slacked off and times when I was very dedicated. But it is *so* rewarding and enjoyable to spend time every day with our Creator, to learn and grow more mature, to experience His love, and to see it on a daily basis.

No matter what's going on in our lives, it's important that you and I keep Jesus as our focus—to love him, love others, and be bold. I hope that you have been encouraged by everything you have read!

Aloha,
Bethany

P.S. I also want to welcome you to check out my website, www.bethanyhamilton.com. Here you can

follow up on the adventures I continue to have, the work I'm doing in Christ's name, and my surfing contests. Please understand that I do get a lot of e-mails (thousands!). Although I would love to respond to them all, I can't. But I do appreciate them all!

Her story is amazing enough to inspire a major motion picture. Back on the surfboard just one month after losing her arm in a shark attack, professional surfer Bethany Hamilton became the cover girl of courage, inspiring millions around the world.

In this devotional, Bethany speaks straight to her "soul sisters," teen girls, about the challenges of facing your fears, living your faith, and letting God take you on an epic ride.

Flip through the pages to read about how to stand up for your faith, make a difference, and avoid wipe-outs. Read Bethany's prayers and then journal your own. Learn about the highs of extreme sports and extreme faith.

A top-ranked p[...] Christian, Bethany Hamilton lives t[...]awaii. She is the best-selling author of *Soul Surfer* and has been featured in *Life*, *Self*, *Time*, *People*, and *Sports Illustrated*. Her story can be seen in the major motion picture *Soul Surfer*.

JUVENILE NONFICTION / Religion / General
$14.99 U.S.
ISBN: 978-1-4003-1723-3

51499

9 781400 317233

THOMAS NELSON
Since 1798

For other products and live events,
visit us at thomasnelson.com